Easy Oracle SQL
*Get Started Fast Writing SQL Reports with SQL*Plus*

Easy Oracle Series

John Garmany

I dedicate this book to my wife, the most important person in my life. All my love.

-- John Garmany

Easy Oracle SQL
*Get Started Fast writing SQL Reports with SQL*Plus*

By John Garmany

Copyright © 2005 by Rampant TechPress. All rights reserved.

Printed in the United States of America.

Easy Oracle Series Book #5

Published by: Rampant TechPress, Kittrell, North Carolina, USA

Production Editor: Teri Wade

Production Manager: Robert Tuttle

Cover Design: Bryan Hoff

Illustrations: Mike Reed

Printing History: April, 2005 for First Edition

ISBN: 0-9727513-7-8

Library of Congress Control Number: 2005901262

Table of Contents

Using the Online Code Depot

Purchase of this book provides complete access to the online code depot that contains the sample code scripts. All of the code depot scripts in this book are located at the following URL:

rampant.cc/easy_sql.htm

All of the code scripts in this book are available for download in zip format, ready to load and use. If technical assistance is needed with downloading or accessing the scripts, please contact Rampant TechPress at info@rampant.cc.

Are you WISE?

Get the premier Oracle tuning tool. The Workload Interface Statistical Engine for Oracle provides unparallel capability for time-series Oracle tuning, available nowhere else.

WISE supplements Oracle Enterprise Manager and it can quickly plot and spot performance signatures to allow you to see hidden trends, fast.

WISE interfaces with STATSPACK or AWR to provide unprecedented proactive tuning insights. Best of all, it is only $9.95 for the Standard Edition and $199.95 for the Enterprise Edition. **Get WISE. Download Now!**

www.wise-oracle.com

Got Scripts?

This is the complete Oracle script collection from Mike Ault and Donald Burleson, the world's best Oracle DBA's.

Packed with over 500 ready-to-use Oracle scripts, this is the definitive collection for every Oracle professional DBA. It would take many years to develop these scripts from scratch, making this download the best value in the Oracle industry.

It's only $39.95 (less than 7 cents per script!). For immediate download go to:

www.oracle-script.com

Conventions Used in this Book

It is critical for any technical publication to follow rigorous standards and employ consistent punctuation conventions to make the text easy to read.

However, this is not an easy task. Within Oracle there are many types of notation that can confuse a reader. Some Oracle utilities such as STATSPACK and TKPROF are always spelled in CAPITAL letters, while Oracle parameters and procedures have varying naming conventions in the Oracle documentation. It is also important to remember that many Oracle commands are case sensitive, and are always left in their original executable form, and never altered with italics or capitalization.

Hence, all Rampant TechPress books follow these conventions:

Parameters - All Oracle parameters will be lowercase italics. Exceptions to this rule are parameter arguments that are commonly capitalized (KEEP pool, TKPROF), these will be left in ALL CAPS.

Variables - All PL/SQL program variables and arguments will also remain in lowercase italics (*dbms_job*, *dbms_utility*).

Tables & dictionary objects – All data dictionary objects are referenced in lowercase italics (*dba_indexes*, *v$sql*). This includes all v$ and x$ views (*x$kcbcbh*, *v$parameter*) and dictionary views (*dba_tables*, *user_indexes*).

SQL - All SQL is formatted for easy use in the code depot. The main SQL terms (select, from, where, group by, order by, having) will always appear on a separate line.

Programs & Products - All products and programs that are known to the author are capitalized according to the vendor specifications (IBM, DBXray, etc). All names known by

Rampant TechPress to be trademark names appear in this text as initial caps. References to UNIX are always made in uppercase.

Acknowledgements

This type of technical reference book requires the dedicated efforts of many people. Even though I am the author, my work ends when I deliver the content.

After each chapter is delivered, several Oracle DBAs carefully review and correct the technical content. The finished work is then reviewed as page proofs and turned over to the production manager, who arranges the creation of the online code depot and manages the cover art, printing distribution, and warehousing.

In short, the author plays a small role in the development of this book, and I need to thank and acknowledge everyone who helped bring this book to fruition:

Robert Tuttle, for the production management, including the coordination of the cover art, page proofing, printing, and distribution.

Teri Wade, for her help in the production of the page proofs.

Bryan Hoff, for his exceptional cover design and graphics.

Janet Burleson, for her assistance with the web site, and for creating the code depot and the online shopping cart for this book.

Linda Webb, for her expert page-proofing services.

Don Burleson, for his expert technical review of the content.

With my sincerest thanks,

John W. Garmany

Preface

Databases have existed virtually since the invention of the computer. Once a machine was built that could process data, a method to store that data was needed, thus the database was created. Today databases can be found on every type and size of computer from the giant mainframes to the small palm pilot and cell phone.

The simplest definition of a database is a collection of data items stored for later retrieval. Basically, the database allows the storage and retrieval of data. When the first caveman used charcoal to etch on the cave wall to track the passage of time, the database was born. Data was stored as marks on the wall and retrieved by looking at the wall. The marks moved from the wall to a notebook, to a filing cabinet, and to data files in a directory on a computer. The databases used today are actually highly specialized applications that not only store and retrieve data, but also protect and secure it.

The first commercial databases, such as the IBM IMS, were developed in the 1960's. They were followed by the Cullinet IDMS database of the 1970's and 1980's. These databases had a very cumbersome interface and it was quite difficult to get data out of the database. One of the largest benefits of the new relational databases of the 1980's was the ability to have a simple data access method called Structured Query Language, or SQL.

All relational database management systems use SQL to access data, and SQL is the defacto standard for database access. Only specialized or object oriented databases do not use SQL. The relational database model is a newcomer. Relational databases took decades to displace the older hierarchical and network database models. Oracle released the first commercial relational database in 1979. Since that time, the relational database has become one of the, if not the, most important business tools.

But databases do far more than just store data. Relational databases also store the relationships between the data, and the relational information is the key. For example, if a customer has placed four orders, this fact is stored in the database engine, right along with the data.

Many companies simply would not exist if they lost the company data stored in their databases. Databases backend most applications used today. Simple things such as checkbook programs or email programs have to store and retrieve significant amounts of data. I have over 1 Gigabyte of emails in my Thunderbird files and have only been using it for a few months. Even my Palm Pilot stores information and applications in a database.

As this data volume grows, easy access becomes more important and problematic. Effectively using SQL will allow the retrieval of the information needed while weeding out that which is not needed.

This book begins with a very short introduction to Entity Relation Diagrams and normalization, followed by a very high level introduction to the Oracle database. After that, the focus of the book is pure SQL. The book begins with the SELECT statements in Chapter 1 and continues to develop its capabilities through Chapter 3. Then Chapter 4 introduces the INSERT, UPDATE and DELETE statements. Finally, Chapter 5 covers how to manage database objects using SQL.

The remainder of this book focuses on SQL for the Oracle database. Oracle implements the ANSI standard SQL plus some enhancements. All relational database vendors want to follow the ANSI SQL standard, but they also want to extend their version of SQL to make their product more appealing than the competitors'!

Almost all SQL in this book will work with other database systems. Many databases do not implement the entire ANSI standard. Some cannot execute subqueries or unions. To get the most from this book it is recommended that you visit otn.oracle.com and download the latest version of the Oracle database, install it and use it to follow along the examples and exercises.

Feedback is always welcome regarding how to improve this book, and you are encouraged to contact me with suggestions at info@rampant.cc

Introduction to the Relational Database

There is no magic to writing SQL

Inside the Relational Model

Relational databases allow a user to both store and retrieve data, manipulating the data into many different forms. Also, relational databases store more than just the data itself and all sorts of other information is stored inside Oracle.

During the development of all computer systems, an important task is designing the database, and placing the data into its proper form:

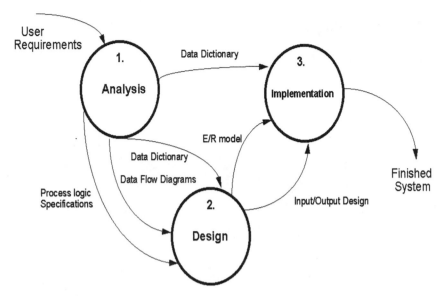

Figure 1.1: *Database design process*

Remember, storing data is not enough and you must capture information about the relationships between the data. That's information, too. Oracle stores all of the following inside the database:

- Data Relationships (using "constraints")

- Application programs (Java and PL/SQL are stored inside "procedures")

- Metadata (data about data) is stored in the data dictionary

- Business logic (the object-oriented tables with methods)

Internally, Oracle stores the data in the lowest form possible to allow for flexible retrieval, and you can expand on the data form inside your SQL query. Let's take a look.

Data is stored inside relational tables. Each table is an entity like an address or a person record. Tables are made up of rows and columns very much like a spreadsheet.

	A	B	C	D	E	F	G
1	YEAR	QTR	MONTH	ORDER #	Salesperson	Customer	Cust-city
2	1994	Q1	Jan	112	Jones	AT&T	Chicago
3	1994	Q1	Jan	112	Jones	AT&T	Chicago
4	1994	Q1	Jan	112	Jones	AT&T	Chicago
5	1994	Q1	Jan	112	Jones	AT&T	Chicago
6	1994	Q1	Feb	343	Smith	IBM	Miami
7	1994	Q1	Feb	343	Smith	IBM	Miami
8	1994	Q1	Feb	343	Smith	IBM	Miami
9	1994	Q1	Feb	343	Smith	ABC Corp	Atlanta
10	1994	Q1	Feb	343	Smith	ABC Corp	Atlanta
11	1994	Q1	Feb	343	Smith	ABC Corp	Atlanta
12	1994	Q1	Feb	343	Smith	ABC Corp	Atlanta
13	1994	Q1	Feb	343	Smith	ABC Corp	Atlanta
14	1994	Q1	Feb	343	Smith	ABC Corp	Atlanta
15	1994	Q1	Feb	411	Bradley	XYZ Inc.	Fresno
16	1994	Q1	Feb	411	Bradley	XYZ Inc.	Fresno
17	1994	Q1	Feb	411	Bradley	XYZ Inc.	Fresno
18	1994	Q1	Feb	411	Bradley	XYZ Inc.	Fresno
19	1994	Q1	Feb	411	Bradley	XYZ Inc.	Fresno
20	1994	Q1	Feb	411	Bradley	XYZ Inc.	Fresno

Figure 1.2: *Sample relational table*

User ID = reader, Password = group

All the columns in a row pertain to the data in only that row. Each row in a table must have a key that uniquely identifies that row. This key is called the table's Primary Key. For example, an ADDRESS table might look like this:

Street	City	ST	Zip
234 Starry Lane	Hereville	FL	34509
793 Davis Street	Thereville	CO	07843
482 MyStreet	Whereville	WO	58372

Table 1.1: *Sample address table*

This table contains three rows. But who lives where? How do I retrieve one of these addresses? First, I need to add a primary key for my ADDRESS table, so I add a key:

Add_key	Street	City	ST	Zip
A100	234 Starry Lane	Hereville	FL	34509
A101	793 Davis Street	Thereville	CO	07843
A102	482 MyStreet	Whereville	WO	58372

Table 1.2: *Sample ADDRESS table with primary key*

Now, when I retrieve the address that corresponds to key A101, I get the Thereville address. My table of friends can now use this key to link names with addresses.

F_Key	FirstName	LastName	Add_key
F100	John	Smith	A100
F101	Sammy	Spade	A101
F102	Thomas	Jones	A102

Table 1.3: *Sample table for linking names with addresses*

Now, I can join my FRIENDS table to my ADDRESS table and see that John Smith lives in Hereville. But wait! Why not place both those items in one table? The answer is: I can. But I may not want to, and in fact I probably don't want to. In this little example, I could easily combine the two tables, but if my example grew large I would run into problems mostly with performance.

If I happen to have two million friends and I decided to throw a party and invite everyone from Hereville, I need to know how many friends I have in Hereville. If I only have one table with all my data in it, I must search through all that data just to count the number of Herevilles.

It is much more efficient to count the number of Herevilles in the smaller address table. Since I don't need my friend's names, why sort through that unnecessary data to get what I need? By separating data into subtables, I can also remove redundancy. If two or more friends have the same address, they will share the same address key. This is called normalizing the data.

Basic SQL

The SQL language has three types of operations that allow you to manipulate the tables in any way you want.

- **Select** – Gets the rows that you want: The select operator shrinks the table vertically. In the example below, the "*" means to select all columns, and the WHERE clause removes rows that we don't want to see:

SELECT

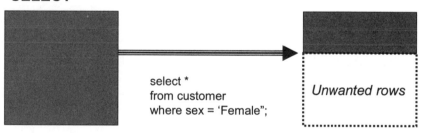

select *
from customer
where sex = 'Female';

Unwanted rows

- **Project** – Chooses the columns you want to see. Shrinks the table horizontally:

PROJECT

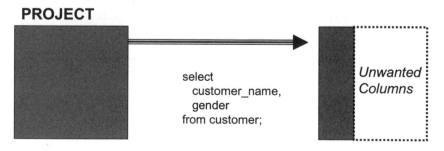

select
    customer_name,
    gender
from customer;

Unwanted Columns

- **Join** – Joins the table together, based on their common keys:

JOIN

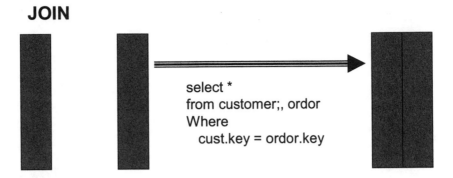

```
select *
from customer;, ordor
Where
    cust.key = ordor.key
```

Now that we understand the basics of tables, let's take a look at how tables are designed. We don't need to know all of the details, but it's important to understand how tables are structured.

Normalizing Data

Designing a database involves a process called normalization where the data model is broken-down according its smallest granularity. Invented by Ted Codd and Chris Date, the term normalization was borrowed from President Richard Nixon normalizing relations with China in the 1970's.

The process of normalizing data breaks the data down into smaller and smaller tables to reduce redundancy and make retrieving and managing that data more efficient. In general, if you find that you have the same data going into multiple rows, you probably need to break that data out into a separate table. Some of the benefits of normalizing your data are:

- Reducing Disk Storage – Since the smaller tables reduce repeating data, the overall database size is smaller.

- Ease of Maintenance – If an item changes, then I can update it in only one place. If my data in not normalized, then I must update every occurrence of that item.

- Reduce I/O – To retrieve the data I need, I will be reading smaller amounts of data from the disk. If my data is not normalized, I must pull all the data from the disk to find the piece that I want.

- Easier Querying – If I store names as "John Garmany" and I want to know how many friends I have with the first name of "John", I have to read the all the names and extract the first name from each name. If I store the first name and last name as separate items, I can search through only the first names.

- Better Security – In a modern relational database, I can allow a user access to only part of the data. I could restrict access to sensitive data such as social security numbers while still allowing access to data regular users need such as names and addresses.

There is a drawback to normalizing a database. Tables must be joined to recreate the whole date set, when needed. As mentioned before, normalization is a process broken up into steps. At the end of each step, you have a normal form. After the first step, you have First Normal Form. The second step produces Second Normal Form. There are six common steps in the normalization process; however, most systems do not go past Third Normal Form. Since this is not a book about normalization, I will introduce the first three normal forms rather quickly and not dwell on too much detail. You don't need more than a simple understanding of normalization to write SQL.

All about Keys

All relational databases require unique keys to identify primary table rows.

A key is required whenever we need to join tables together with SQL. In most cases, the key will be a unique value (e.g. social security number), but we may sometimes see non-unique key values.

Sometimes the table will not have a unique value, and your table will have a sequence to uniquely identify each table row.

We need these matching keys to use SQL to join tables, and we do this inside our SQL WHERE clause. However, Oracle also has the ability to hard link related rows together. This is Oracle's object oriented feature, where Object ID's are used instead of keys:

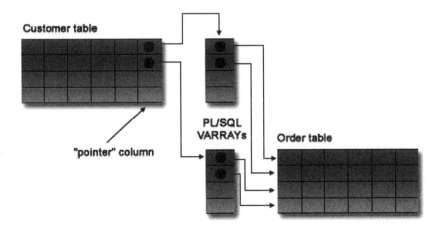

Figure 1.3: *Basic SQL structure*

Now that we see the basics of SQL, let's take a look at the normalization steps, so that we can understand table structure.

Un-normalized Form (0NF)

Essentially, an un-normalized relation is a relation that contains repeating values. An un-normalized relation can also contain relations nested within other relations, as well as all kinds of transitive dependencies. Sometimes un-normalized relations are signified by 0NF, but an un-normalized relation is not to be confused with a denormalized relation.

The un-normalized relation is any relation in its raw state, and they commonly contain repeating vales and other characteristics that are not found in denormalized relations. The process of denormalization is a very deliberate attempt to introduce controlled redundant items into an already normalized form.

First Normal Form (1NF)

In essence, any relation is in first normal form if it does not contain any repeating values. Here, we have taken our relations with repeating values and moved them to separate relations. When the new relations are created, we carry the primary key of the original relation into the new relation.

We start by creating a primary key to uniquely identify each row in the table. Any repeating data is moved to a new table. Finally, create a key for each of the rows of the new table and a reference to that key in the original table. This is like what we did with the FRIENDS and ADDRESS tables above. First normal form removes repeating data to separate tables. Each of the new tables may have repeating data that should be move to another new table. This process continues until there is no longer redundant data.

Second Normal Form (2NF)

For second normal form, you must start in first normal form. Then, each column in a table must be dependent on the key for that table, or it should be move to a new table.

The purpose of the second normal form (2NF) test is to check for partial key dependencies. Partial key dependencies are created when we break off an un-normalized relation into first normal form by carrying the key thereby creating a concatenated key with several data items. The formal definition of second normal form is as follows:

A relation is in second normal form if and only if the relation is in first normal form and each non-key attribute is fully functionally dependent on the entire concatenated key.

However, I prefer the following definition:

A relation is in second normal form if each attribute depends on the key, the whole key, and nothing but the key, so help me Codd.

Third Normal Form (3NF)

The third normal form (3NF) test refers to transitive dependencies. A transitive dependency is a circumstance where one non-key attribute is functionally dependent on another non-key attribute. Whereas the 2NF test serves to check for dependencies between key fields and attribute fields, the 3NF test serves to check for dependencies between non-key attributes.

First, your relation must already be in second normal form. Any column that is dependent on another column that is not the key

---

must be placed in a new table. Any column that is derived from another column (like a total) must be placed in a separate table.

The process of going to 3NF is all about eliminating redundant data inside tables. However, almost all databases are not in 3NF, and your tables will almost always have deliberately-introduced values in multiple tables! Let's see why.

Denormalization

Now that you have an idea of how normalization is used to segregate redundant and non-dependent data, I have to admit that most databases are not all the way into third normal form. As database software had become more powerful and hardware less expensive (such as fast hard drives), many databases are denormalized to improve performance. The process of denormalization has to do with taking a normalized database and reintroducing selected redundancy to improve performance.

When normalization techniques were created, disks were very expensive, and you did not want to have any redundant data because it was very expensive. Since the 1970's, disk have become thousands of times cheaper, and it is now common to go to third normal form and then go back and reintroduce redundant data!

Having data in more than one place can reduce the amount of SQL table joins, making our SQL run faster. The rules for denormalization relate to the size of the data item, and how frequently the data is updated:

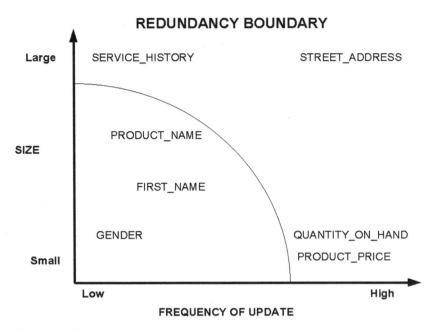

Figure 1.4: *Rules for denormalization*

In other words, a tiny data item that is seldom updated is a great candidate for denormalization. Below, we see a database model where redundant data items have been re-added to eliminate SQL table joins:

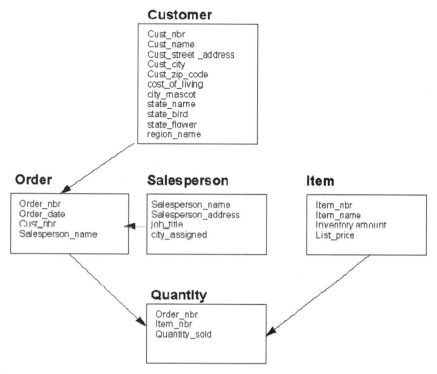

Figure 1.5: *Database model*

The greater the amount of duplicated data, the smaller the number of tables, and the faster the SQL will run.

Aggregation Denormalization

In Oracle data warehouses, tables might have millions of rows, and SQL queries might take hours to run. To solve this problem, Oracle has a tool called a materialized view to pre-summarize data and pre-join table together.

Preaggregation of Oracle data

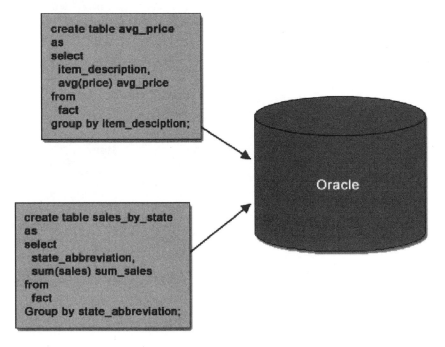

Figure 1.6: *Preaggregation of data*

When you pre-summarize data with materialized views, you don't need to change your SQL! Oracle has a super-cool feature called query re-write where Oracle will automatically know when your SQL can use a pre-summarized result.

So, I have my data, and I want to start building my database. How can I visualize my data and go through the normalization process with out constantly recreating the database? For this, you want to use the Entity Relation Diagram.

Entity Relation Modeling

Data modeling is a method for developing the structure of the database. It uses various tools to define the data, relationships, semantics and data consistency requirements. The Entity Relation Diagram (ERD) is where most designers start when creating and normalizing a database. An ERD normally starts on paper with a general layout of the database data entities and their relationships.

The entity/relation model was first introduced by Professor Emeritus Peter Chen from the University of Louisiana, and it is sometimes called a Chen diagram. In the 25 years since the introduction of this model, many permutations have been created, but the basic principles of entity/relations modeling remain intact.

While an E/R model may be free of redundant information, it is impossible to implement the model in a relational database without introducing redundancy to support the data relationships. For example, if a data model was implemented using a pointer-based DBMS, such as IMS, pointers would be used to establish relationships between entities.

At some point, the diagram becomes unwieldy on paper and an ERD tool is used to graphically finish the design. In a nutshell, the ER diagram shows the data tables, and more importantly, it shows the one-to-many and many-to-many data relationships:

First, all employees are going to be in a department, so the *dept* attribute will have a lot of redundant information in it. Also, the department is not dependent on the *emp_num* key, so we need to split it out into its own entity. Secondly, you might want to use the social security number (*ssn*) as the primary key; however, this will limit your design to just persons with a *ssn*. No persons from other countries, since they will not have a *ssn*. Finally, employee name should be broken up into subelements such as first, middle initial and last name. After incorporating the changes, we now have the diagram in Figure 1.9.

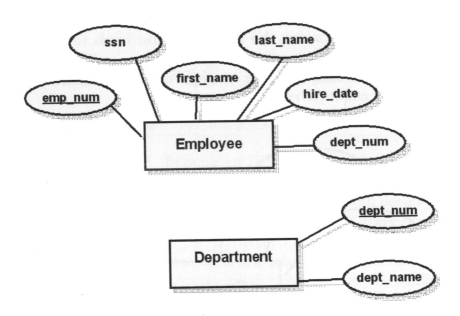

Figure 1.9: *Redrawn Employee Entity*

Notice that department is now its own entity with the *dept_num* as the primary key. Also notice that we place a *dep_num* attribute in the employee entity, this is know as a Foreign Key. It is an attribute that references another entity's primary key (more on that in Chapter 5). This actually defines a relationship between the employee and the department entity.

But, I am ahead of myself. Entities can be a type of another entity. An employee is also a person. If I have a person entity, the employee would be a subtype of the person entity. For now, we will stick with the employee type.

Inside Data Relationships

As we know, the data relationships associate the entities with each other and allow us to join them together. Initially in the ERD, relationships are defined with words.

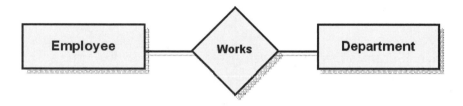

Figure 1.10: *Employee Department Relationship*

In Figure 1.10, the employee entity works in a department entity. Links are defined as to the cardinality of the entities in the relationship. For example, an employee can only work in zero or one department. The link between the employee and the department is a one-to-one (or one-to-none).

A department can have many employees, so the relationship between departments and employees is one-to-many (one dept, many employees). If an employee could be in more than one department, then the link would be many-to-many. Each tool uses a method of defining the cardinality of a link. Here are some examples in Figure 1.11.

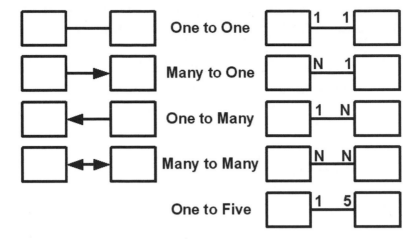

Figure 1.11: *Link Cardinality*

Weak Entities

Weak entities have no physical value. They are used to solve the problem created by a many-to-many link. Since each relationship must have a unique identifier, the many-to-many link must be broken up to one-to-many links.

The weak entity is used for this purpose. It uses one of the primary keys as an attribute. For example, an individual can have many hobbies; many individuals can have a particular hobby. Thus, the link shown in figure 1.12 is many-to-many. By adding a weak entity and relationship, I convert the link to a one-to-one between an individual and a list of hobbies, and a one-to-many between the list of hobbies and a hobby.

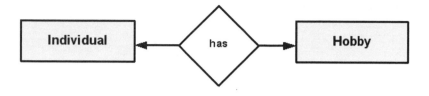

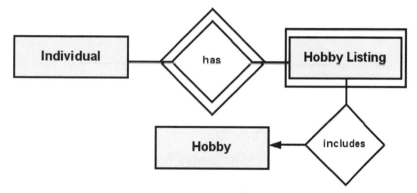

Figure 1.12: *Weak Entity*

So, an individual can have only one list of hobbies. The list of hobbies can contain one or more hobbies. Weak entities can contain attributes and will become a table in the database once the design is completed.

Misleading data Relationships

If we follow the formal rules for entity relational modeling, it is tempting to move all relations into separate tables. For example, we might note:

- Each city has many zip codes – A zip code belongs to only one city

- People have many hair colors – Any person has only one hair color

Misleading data relatioships

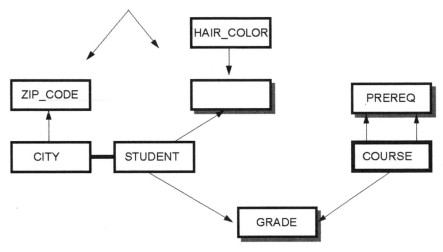

Figure 1.13: *Misleading data relationships*

It would be tempting to create tables for zip code and hair color, but this is incorrect! It is wrong because there are no additional attributes to zip code and hair color. Remember, the smaller the number of tables, the faster your SQL will run!

The PUBS Database

For the remainder of the book, we will be using the PUBS database. This database was designed as a teaching tool and is available in the code depot.

The file is simply a list of commands that creates and populates the database. We will learn each of the commands as we continue through this text.

Installing the PUBS database creates a user called *pubs* and grants the role of DBA to that user. As such, this script should only be used in a training/test/development environment.

To install the PUBS database, you need a running Oracle database. Here, we assume that you have already installed the Oracle database. When the database was created, you assigned it a *sid*. Copy the PUBS.sql file to a practice directory.

Start the database.

On Windows, go to services, right click and start the service OracleService<SID>. Then, start the service OracleListener.

On Linux/Unix, you must set the environmental variables Oracle Home and Oracle SID before starting the database. Substitute the correct information in the example below.

```
$ export ORACLE_HOME=/opt/oracle
$ export ORACLE_SID=mydb
$ sqlplus "/ as sysdba"
SQL> startup
SQL> exit
$ lsnrctl start
```

In both cases, we started two programs, the database and the listener. The listener listens on a port (normally 1521, but you can change the port) for a connection. When you connect to the database, the listener takes your connection request and creates a server process to perform the actual database work. We will learn more about the database later in this chapter.

Open a terminal window and change into the practice directory.

On Windows select Start – Run – type cmd and press enter. On Linux, right click on the desktop and select terminal.

Change to the working directory:

```
C:> cd c:\john
$ cd john
```

All the examples in this book will use SQL*Plus. This is Oracle's command line tool for interacting with the database. We will go into SQL*Plus in much more detail later. Start SQL*Plus as the super user.

```
$ sqlplus "/ as sysdba"
SQL>
```

After starting, SQL*Plus will leave you at the SQL> prompt. To load the PUBS database, you will need to run the PUBS.sql script.

```
SQL> @pubs.sql
```

This will create the PUBS user with a password of pubs, create the tables and load the data. When you are through, you will be left as the user PUBS. You can verify this with the command below:

```
SQL> show user
PUBS
SQL> exit
```

Use exit to get back to the operating system prompt.

The Code Depot also contains a PowerPoint slide (PUBS.ppt) with the diagram of the PUBS database. The PUBS database details information about publishing books. There is an author table which list authors. Notice that it contains a unique key called the *auth_key* that uniquely identifies each author. The book table list books. The store table list stores that sell the books and the sales table list books sold, by order number, in each store. A publisher also has employees who, of course, print the books. You can see the links between each table. Notice the *book_author* table. Remember, the weak entity needed to eliminate the many-to-many link. An author can write many books, and a book can have more than one author. The *book_author* table eliminates that many-to-many link. The primary key in the *book_author* table is both the *auth_key* and the *book_key* (a multicolumn key).

Before we jump into using SQL, we need to know a little about how the Oracle database handles our request.

Inside the Oracle Database

The Oracle database is made up of a large shared chunk of memory and multiple processes that support that memory. The memory contains the buffer cache, library cache, data dictionary, and some other items. The buffer cache is where all the work on the data is done. Before data is read, updated, created or deleted it is moved to the buffer cache. Also, in this chunk of shared memory is a pool called the shared pool. The shared pool contains the library cache and the data dictionary cache. The library cache is where the database stores plans to execute SQL that it has received. If the same SQL is resubmitted, it can use the plan in the library cache to quickly execute the request. The data dictionary cache (also in the shared pool) is where the database caches database metadata (data about the data that makes up the database). Figure 1.15 shows these memory structures.

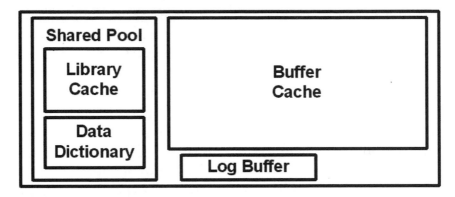

Figure 1.15: *Oracle Memory Structures*

There are actually a number of other structures in that shared memory, but these are the ones we are interested in. All of the caches in the database use some form of "least recently used" caching algorithm. If the database needs to read data into the buffer cache and it is full, it will remove the data that has not been used the longest and read in the new data. Likewise, if you submit a SQL request and there is no room in the library cache, you will force the least use SQL to age out of the cache to make room for your statement.

One buffer that we have not yet discussed is the Log Buffer. This buffer, along with the undo log files, holds information about changes to data. They are used to provide users with a consistent view.

Consistent View

A consistent view is a very important concept, and how it works is different depending on which database software you are using. Oracle implements a consistent view that basically says that a user will see only committed data. It sounds easy, but it is actually one of the features that sets Oracle apart from other database systems. The key to understanding a consistent view is understanding what and when data changes are committed.

If I was in charge of the payroll and needed to give everyone a 10% raise, I could create a query that will do that. Once the query was run, everyone's pay rate would equal (payrate * .10). If I queried your pay rate, I would see your new pay rate. This change is not yet permanent. To make it permanent, I need to issue a commit. This tells the database to make the change permanent. If I made a mistake, I could issue the command to rollback and the data would be returned to the point before I gave everyone the raise. The thing to note is that once I commit, I can no longer rollback.

Now, where does the consistent view come in? Let's go back to the example. I give everyone a pay raise but have not committed. When I query the data, I will see everyone having the new pay rate. When you query your pay rate, it will be the original pay rate. Why? Because I have not committed the change, so Oracle will not show the changes to anyone but me. Once I commit, your query will return the new pay rate. This is the key point; Oracle will never show uncommitted data to anyone other than the user that made the change. What happens when I change your pay rate (add 10%) and you change your pay rate (+15%) and neither one of us commits? We both changed the same piece of data. I will see the 10% raise while you will see the 15% raise. If I commit, my change will become permanent, but you will still see the 15% raise. If someone else queries the data, they will see my 10% raise. If you then commit, everyone will see the 15% pay raise. Thus, you will see your own changes but no one else will see them until you commit. When multiple users are changing the same data, he who commits last wins! Some database programs will allow you to see others' uncommitted data. This is called a dirty read. Oracle will not allow dirty reads. How Oracle implements this is complicated, but basically, the database records changes in the buffer cache, log buffer and undo logs. When I make a change, the change is stored in the buffer cache and the undo is stored in the undo logs. If I rollback the change, the data in the undo logs are used to return the data to its original state. If I have not committed my change and you read the data, Oracle sees that the data has changed but is not committed, and it uses the undo data to recreate the original data for you. Bottom line is that you will never see someone else's uncommitted data.

SQL and SQL*Plus

So, we started our database and loaded the PUBS schema. Now, let's dive into SQL (pronounced sequel). Relational databases and SQL were developed in the early 1970s at IBM. SQL stands for Structured Query Language. The idea was to define a common method of storing data that would allow you to retrieve specific information without detailed knowledge of the underlying database engine. In 1979, Oracle released the first commercial relational database that used SQL. In 1986, the American National Standards Institute (ANSI) began publishing SQL standards. SQL is currently the standard query method of all major database management systems. In Oracle, SQL is divided into two basic groups: data definition language (DDL) or data manipulation language (DML). DDL is used to define objects within the database just as creating tables or indexes. DML is used to insert, update and delete data in the database. Finally, there is data retrieval, which is the SELECT statement.

The examples in this book are created using SQL*Plus. SQL*Plus is the command line interface to the Oracle Database. The first step is to start SQL*Plus and connect to the database. In Windows, open a terminal window. In Linux/Unix go to the command line and ensure that the database environment is set.

To start SQL*Plus just enter "sqlplus". If the program is not found, make sure the ORACLE_HOME is set in the path.

```
[oracle@appsvr oracle]$ sqlplus
SQL*Plus: Release 10.1.0.2.0 - Production on Thu Jan 20 20:23:44 2005
Copyright (c) 1982, 2004, Oracle.  All rights reserved.
Enter user-name:
```

My database is called DEVDB. I can start SQL*Plus and log on in one command like below.

```
[oracle@appsvr oracle]$ sqlplus pubs/pubs@devdb
SQL*Plus: Release 10.1.0.2.0 - Production on Thu Jan 20 20:28:11 2005
Copyright (c) 1982, 2004, Oracle.  All rights reserved.
Connected to:
Oracle Database 10g Enterprise Edition Release 10.1.0.2.0 - Production
With the Partitioning, OLAP and Data Mining options
SQL>
```

The log on format is:

```
username/password@database_service_name.
```

The database service name is the name of the entry in the TNSNAMES.ora file located in the ORACLE_HOME/ network/admin/tnsnames.ora. You may need to get with your DBA to setup the TNSNAME.ORA file. If you are running SQL*Plus on the computer that you installed Oracle on, the installation program created a TNSNAMES entry that matches the database name, in my case DEVDB.

If there was someone watching me log on and I didn't want them to see my password, I could not included it and SQL*Plus will ask for it and not echo the password to the screen.

```
[oracle@appsvr oracle]$ sqlplus pubs@devdb
SQL*Plus: Release 10.1.0.2.0 - Production on Thu Jan 20 20:29:54 2005
Copyright (c) 1982, 2004, Oracle.  All rights reserved.
Enter password:
Connected to:
Oracle Database 10g Enterprise Edition Release 10.1.0.2.0 - Production
With the Partitioning, OLAP and Data Mining options
SQL>
```

Now that we are connected, lets get to the SQL. I would recommend that you print a copy of the pubs.ppt slide in the Code Depot for easy reference. Look at the AUTHOR table. You can also see what makes up the AUTHOR table by describing it.

```
SQL> desc author

Name                                    Null?    Type
--------------------------------------- -------- ------------
AUTHOR_KEY                                       VARCHAR2(11)
AUTHOR_LAST_NAME                                 VARCHAR2(40)
AUTHOR_FIRST_NAME                                VARCHAR2(20)
AUTHOR_PHONE                                     VARCHAR2(12)
AUTHOR_STREET                                    VARCHAR2(40)
AUTHOR_CITY                                      VARCHAR2(20)
AUTHOR_STATE                                     VARCHAR2(2)
AUTHOR_ZIP                                       VARCHAR2(5)
AUTHOR_CONTRACT_NBR                              NUMBER(5)
```

This command lists the columns and their definitions.

SQL*Plus places each command into a buffer. You can edit the SQL*Plus buffer, but it is more efficient to create and run scripts (unless you are a vi cowboy) (if you don't know what that is don't worry, you are not one). When you enter a command, SQL*Plus will continue to place it into the buffer until it encounters a semicolon. This tells SQL*Plus to execute the command. You can re-execute the previous command by entering a forward slash (/) or by entering RUN. To list the current buffer enter "L". When you enter a carriage return without a semicolon, SQL*Plus assumes you are still entering a command and will provide another line. The Windows version of SQL*Plus also has a command history that you can cycle through using the Up/Down arrows.

As your queries become more complicated, you will want to be able to edit your queries. The easiest way to do this is to use the host command. Enter host notepad <filename> at the SQL prompt to open a text file in notepad. Write/edit the query, save and close the file, then execute it with the @<filename> command. To re-edit the file, hit the up arrow to bring the host command back, enter and edit the query. In this way, you can quickly go from editing to execution and back to editing.

The SELECT statement

The SELECT statement is used to retrieve data from the database. The format is:

```
select columns from tables;
```

Let's get a list of author last names.

```
SQL> SELECT author_last_name FROM author;

AUTHOR_LAST_NAME
----------------------------------------
jones
hester
weaton
jeckle
withers
petty
clark
mee
shagger
smith

10 rows selected.
```

In SQL*Plus, statements sent to the database must end with a semicolon. SQL*Plus will continue to add lines to the buffer until it get a semicolon. The command below will give the same results. Notice that if you press ENTER and there is no semicolon, SQL*Plus assumes that you are entering another line.

```
SQL> SELECT
  2    author_last_name
  3  FROM
  4    author;
```

```
AUTHOR_LAST_NAME
----------------------------------------
jones
hester
weaton
jeckle
withers
petty
clark
mee
shagger
smith

10 rows selected.
```

This is important because formatting commands will help you avoid errors. As our queries become more complicated, formatting becomes more important. If I want to retrieve more than one column, I list them, separated by a comma. The order that I list the columns in the query will be the order that they are returned.

```
SQL> SELECT
  2     author_last_name,
  3     author_first_name,
  4     author_city
  5  FROM
  6     author;

AUTHOR_LAST_NAME                         AUTHOR_FIRST_NAME
----------------------------------------  --------------------
AUTHOR_CITY
--------------------
jones                                    mark
st. louis

hester                                   alvis
st. louis

weaton                                   erin
st. louis
```

```
AUTHOR_LAST_NAME                              AUTHOR_FIRST_NAME
-------------------------------------------   -------------------
AUTHOR_CITY
-------------------
jeckle                                        pierre
north hollywood

withers                                       lester
pie town

petty                                         juan
happyville


AUTHOR_LAST_NAME                              AUTHOR_FIRST_NAME
-------------------------------------------   -------------------
AUTHOR_CITY
-------------------
clark                                         louis
rose garden

mee                                           minnie
belaire

shagger                                       dirk
cross trax


AUTHOR_LAST_NAME                              AUTHOR_FIRST_NAME
-------------------------------------------   -------------------
AUTHOR_CITY
-------------------
smith                                         diego
tweedle


10 rows selected.
```

We will get to cleaning up the output in a moment. First a few points about queries.

- SQL is not case sensitive. I placed the key words in caps, but that is not a requirement. Case is important when we get to actual data, but only for the data. In other words, if I query looking for "John", then "JOHN" and "john" will not be returned.

- Formatting makes the query more readable to humans; it has no effect on the results or the performance. Tabs can be used to indent; however, some programs do not play well with tabs so it is best to just indent with spaces.

- Oracle stores database metadata (table names, index names, etc) in upper case. User data is stored as it is entered.

At this point, let's jump to the SALES table and do some work with numbers. First, describe the table.

```
SQL> desc sales
 Name                                      Null?    Type
 ----------------------------------------- -------- ------------
 STORE_KEY                                          VARCHAR2(4)
 BOOK_KEY                                           VARCHAR2(6)
 ORDER_NUMBER                                       VARCHAR2(20)
 ORDER_DATE                                         DATE
 QUANTITY                                           NUMBER(5)
```

Now, retrieve a list of *order_numbers* and quantities.

```
SQL> SELECT
  2     order_number,
  3     quantity
FROM
  sales;

ORDER_NUMBER           QUANTITY
-------------------- ----------
O101                       1000
O102                         10
O103                        200
O104                        400
O105                        800
O106                        180
O107                        900
.....
O198                       8900
O199                       8800

ORDER_NUMBER           QUANTITY
-------------------- ----------
O200                        100

100 rows selected.
```

I cut out the middle part of the result set. Notice that the character column is left justified and the number column is right justified. This is how SQL*Plus returns the data. I can also change the column heading by aliasing the columns. You can alias a column using the AS keyword, or you can leave it out. If your new column name includes a space, you need to enclose the alias in quotes.

```
SQL> SELECT
  2     order_number AS "Order Number",
  3     quantity qty
  4   FROM
  5     sales;

Order Number                QTY
-------------------- ----------
O101                       1000
O102                         10
O103                        200
O104                        400
O105                        800
O106                        180
   . . .
```

If I wanted to select all the columns, I would "select * from sales".

```
SQL> SELECT * FROM sales;

STOR BOOK_K ORDER_NUMBER       ORDER_DAT  QUANTITY
---- ------ -------------------- --------- ----------
S101 B101   O101                 02-JAN-02      1000
S102 B102   O102                 02-JAN-02        10
S103 B102   O103                 02-JAN-02       200
S104 B102   O104                 03-JAN-02       400
S105 B102   O105                 03-JAN-02       800
S106 B103   O106                 03-JAN-02       180
S107 B103   O107                 04-JAN-02       900
  .    .   .
```

You can also do math on number columns. Math in SQL follows the normal order of precedence. Multiplication (*) and Division (/) before Addition (+) and Subtraction (-). Operators of the same priority are evaluated left to right. Use parentheses to change the order of evaluation.

```
SQL> SELECT
  2     order_number Ord,
  3     quantity,
  4     2*quantity+10 num
  5  FROM
  6     sales;

ORD                           QUANTITY        NUM
-------------------------    ----------   ----------
O101                              1000         2010
O102                                10           30
O103                               200          410
O104                               400          810
O105                               800         1610
 .  .  .
```

Notice in the example above that the multiplication happened before the addition. A NULL values is a column value that has not been assigned or has been set to NULL. It is not a blank space or a zero. It is undefined. Because a NULL is undefined, there is no such thing as NULL math. A NULL + 4 = NULL. NULL * 3 = NULL. Since NULL is undefined, all math using a NULL returns a NULL.

The Data Dictionary - Finding Data in the Database

Since we have the pubs.ppt slide, it is easy to see what each table in our schema consists of. If we didn't have the slide, we could describe the tables to find out what makes up the tables. But what if we didn't know which tables are in the PUBS schema? Oracle provides views that allow us to query this information from the database.

In Oracle, a view is a pseudo-table that is created when a query is run against it. In other words, there is no table called *user_tables*. When I query my *table_names* from *user_tables*, Oracle temporarily creates the table to answer the query. There are three levels of views:

- The **USER** View - The *user* view will return those items that you own. Your tables, indexes, sequences etc.

- The **ALL** View – The *all* view will return those objects that you own and those objects that you have been granted rights on. If another schema has granted *select* on one of their tables to you (the PUBS user), then it will appear in the all views. It will not appear in the user view.

- The **DBA** View – The *dba* view returns all objects in the database.

If an object exists but is not returned in the view you use, the database returns an "object does not exits" error. This is a security feature, because if you are not granted access to it, you are not allowed to know it exists.

To get a list of the PUBS tables, we query the *user_tables* view.

```
SQL> desc user_tables;

Name                                     Null?    Type
---------------------------------------- -------- ----------------
--------
TABLE_NAME                               NOT NULL VARCHAR2(30)
TABLESPACE_NAME                                   VARCHAR2(30)
CLUSTER_NAME                                      VARCHAR2(30)
IOT_NAME                                          VARCHAR2(30)
 .   .   .
```

We are looking for the table names.

```
SQL> SELECT
  2     table_name
  3   FROM
  4     user_tables;

TABLE_NAME
------------------------------
AUTHOR
EMP
JOB
PUBLISHER
SALES
STORE
BOOK_AUTHOR
BOOK
```

To find all the tables we have access to, use the *all* view. The difference between the *user_tables* view and the *all_tables/dba_tables* view is the addition of the *owner* column. Since the *user* view only shows us our own tables, there is no need for the *owner* column. Now, select the *table_name* from the *all_tables* view. Wow! I got 1515 tables (you may get a different number depending on the features you installed in the database). If I query the table names from the *dba_tables* view, I get the same number. This is because we granted the user PUBS the DBA role. Since a DBA has access to all objects in the database, the *all_tables* and *dba_tables* are the same.

There are many *user/all/dba* views, and we will introduce more of them as we progress. Almost all objects have a view: *user_indexes, user_sequences,* etc.

Formatting Output in SQL*Plus

So far, the results returned by our queries have been unformatted and pretty bad looking. What we need to do is format the results. It is important to realize that you are formatting the results in SQL*Plus, not the database. The database just returns the answer; SQL*Plus formats what you see.

The difference between a SQL*Plus command and a query is that the SQL*Plus command does not end in a semicolon. To see the current settings of SQL*Plus' parameters, enter "show all". Most items we will leave at the default. Below is a listing of some of the important parameters that we will need to set to format our output.

- *pages* or *pagesize* – this parameter determines how many lines SQL*Plus will print to the screen before starting a new page and reprinting the column headings. To turn off column headings, set *pages* to zero. To have the column headings appear only once, set *pages* very high (pages 999). *pages* defaults to 14.

- *line* or *linesize* – determines how long a line is. It defaults to 80 characters.

- *feedback* – This is the comment at the end of your listing that tells you how many rows were returned. If you turn feedback off, and your query returns 0 rows, you will simply return to the SQL prompt.

- *trims* or *trimspool* – normally SQL*Plus will fill out a column with blank spaces. *trimspool* causes SQL*Plus to not fill spaces at the end of a line when spooling the results.

All of the commands above are changed using the SET command.

```
SQL> set pages 999 line 132 feedback off
```

Notice that I did not end the line with a semicolon. You can, but it is not necessary since the commands are not sent to the database.

To get a list of SQL*Plus commands type "help index".

```
SQL> help index

Enter Help [topic] for help.

@               COPY          PAUSE                   SHUTDOWN
@@              DEFINE        PRINT                   SPOOL
/               DEL           PROMPT                  SQLPLUS
ACCEPT          DESCRIBE      QUIT                    START
APPEND          DISCONNECT    RECOVER                 STARTUP
ARCHIVE LOG     EDIT          REMARK                  STORE
ATTRIBUTE       EXECUTE       REPFOOTER               TIMING
BREAK           EXIT          REPHEADER               TTITLE
BTITLE          GET           RESERVED WORDS (SQL)    UNDEFINE
CHANGE          HELP          RESERVED WORDS (PL/SQL) VARIABLE
CLEAR           HOST          RUN                     WHENEVER
OSERROR
COLUMN          INPUT         SAVE                    WHENEVER
SQLERROR
COMPUTE         LIST          SET
CONNECT         PASSWORD      SHOW
```

For more detail use "help <command>"

```
SQL> help column

COLUMN
------

Specifies display attributes for a given column, such as:
     - text for the column heading
     - alignment for the column heading
     - format for NUMBER data
     - wrapping of column data
Also lists the current display attributes for a single column
or all columns.

COL[UMN] [{column | expr} [option ...] ]

where option represents one of the following clauses:
     ALI[AS] alias
     CLE[AR]
     ENTMAP {ON|OFF}
     FOLD_A[FTER]
     FOLD_B[EFORE]
     FOR[MAT] format
     HEA[DING] text
     JUS[TIFY] {L[EFT] | C[ENTER] | R[IGHT]}
     LIKE {expr | alias}
     NEWL[INE]
     NEW_V[ALUE] variable
     NOPRI[NT] | PRI[NT]
     NUL[L] text
     OLD_V[ALUE] variable
     ON|OFF
     WRA[PPED] | WOR[D_WRAPPED] | TRU[NCATED]
```

Lets go through some of the more used SQL*Plus commands.

The SPOOL Command

The SPOOL command causes SQL*Plus to write the results to a file.

```
SQL> spool /tmp/myfile.lst
```

Once spool is set, it will continue to spool the output until the command SPOOL OFF. Note that the file cannot be seen or used until the SPOOL OFF command.

@

The @ command tells SQL*Plus to execute a file. The @@ command is used to run a nested script that is located in the same directory as the outer scripts. You can run a nested script with the @ command, but you must fully qualify the file name.

The COLUMN Command

The COLUMN command is used to format the output of a column. Once set it will format any column of that name until it is unset with the CLEAR COLUMNS command.

The TTITLE Command

The TTITLE command sets a title that is printed at the top of each page. Remember that "set pages" defines the page size. If you justify a title, it will be located according to the "set line" command. To change a title, redefine it with the TTITLE command or turn it off (TTITLE OFF).

The HOST Command

The HOST command allows you to run operating system commands. To get a listing of the files in the current directory use:

```
SQL> host dir       Windows
SQL> host ls        Linux/Unix
```

Typing commands at the SQL> prompt is problematic if you type as badly as I do. I want to type in a text editor without leaving SQL*Plus. The host command allows me to do just that.

```
SQL> host notepad test.sql
SQL> host vi test.sql
```

Now I can edit my script using host, and then run it using @.

Let's put all this to work. My boss, the publisher, wants a list of authors (first and last name) and their city. Because it is for my boss, I want the report to look professional. If I simply query the data, it is almost unreadable as seen below.

```
SQL>   SELECT
   2      author_first_name,
   3      author_last_name,
   4      author_city
   5   FROM
   6      author;

AUTHOR_FIRST_NAME     AUTHOR_LAST_NAME
--------------------  ----------------------------------------
AUTHOR_CITY
--------------------
mark                  jones
st. louis

alvis                 hester
st. louis

erin                  weaton
st. louis

pierre                jeckle
north hollywood

lester                withers
pie town

juan                  petty
happyville

louis                 clark
rose garden

minnie                mee
belaire

dirk                  shagger
cross trax

diego                 smith
tweedle


10 rows selected.
```

Now let's fix this up and make it look nice. First we need to fix and size the columns. I am going to alias the columns to *c1*,*c2* and *c3*. Then, use the COLUMN command to format each column. I use the HOST command to open my text editor. I create a file called *auth.sql*. Note the first line. Two dashes define a comment and are ignored by SQL*Plus.

```
-- auth.sql

column c1 heading "First Name" Format a15
column c2 heading Last|Name    Format a30
column c3 heading City         Format a20

 SELECT
   author_first_name c1,
   author_last_name c2,
   author_city c3
 FROM
   author;
```

Once I aliased the column names, the database will return the results using the *c1*, *c2*, *c3* names. I then use the COLUMN command to configure my output. The heading simply names the column much the same as an alias would.

The first column heading has a space in it, so I have to enclose it in quotes. The second heading has a vertical bar which tell SQL*Plus to stack the name (see result below). Finally, I use the FORMAT command to define how many characters wide the column is. If you define the column width smaller that the text returned, the text is wrapped within that column. Below are the results of running my script.

```
SQL>  @auth.sql
              Last
First Name    Name                            City
------------- ------------------------------- --------------------
mark          jones                           st. louis
alvis         hester                          st. louis
erin          weaton                          st. louis
pierre        jeckle                          north hollywood
lester        withers                         pie town
juan          petty                           happyville
louis         clark                           rose garden
minnie        mee                             belaire
dirk          shagger                         cross trax
diego         smith                           tweedle

10 rows selected.
```

The FORMAT command used above determined the width of my columns. But what if I return a number? You define the size of a number using the number nine and zero. The number nine says if there is a digit in that location then print it, if not then print nothing. The number zero says that if there is a digit in that location then print it, otherwise print a zero.

```
Format 9999
    2345            prints      2345
    2345.432        prints      2345
    23456           prints      ####  too large.

Format 9999.00
    2345            prints      2345.00
    2345.432        prints      2345.43
```

If the number exceeds the size of the format, you get pound signs. Since SQL*Plus can't give you the correct number, it gives you nothing.

But, the boss wanted the authors as last name, comma, first name, then city. This is accomplished using concatenation (||). To get this, I need to concatenate three items, last name, the comma, and the first name.

```
-- auth2.sql

column c1 heading Name Format a30
column c2 heading City Format a20
```

```
SELECT
  author_last_name||', '||author_first_name c1,
  author_city c3
FROM
  author;
```

```
SQL>  @auth2.sql

Name                                City
----------------------------------  --------------------
jones, mark                         st. louis
hester, alvis                       st. louis
weaton, erin                        st. louis
jeckle, pierre                      north hollywood
withers, lester                     pie town
petty, juan                         happyville
clark, louis                        rose garden
mee, minnie                         belaire
shagger, dirk                       cross trax
smith, diego                        tweedle

10 rows selected.
```

Don't forget to include any spaces you desire inside the single quotes. We will use these formatting commands throughout this book, focusing on producing readable, professional output.

SQL*Plus Variables

Sometimes you want to run a query over and over again with different data. SQL*Plus provide two methods to pass variables to your query. These are called SQL*Plus variables because the database never sees them. SQL*Plus makes the substitution before sending the query to the database. You define a SQL*Plus variable using the ampersand (&) followed by a name. When SQL*Plus encounters the ampersand, it will ask for the value.

```
SQL> SELECT
  2    author_last_name "Last Name"
  3  FROM
  4    author
  5  WHERE
  6    author_state = &state;
```

```
Enter value for state: 'MO'
old    6:    author_state = &state
new    6:    author_state = 'MO'

Last Name
----------------------------------------
jones
hester
weaton
```

Notice that SQL*Plus shows you the old and new line in the
buffer where the variable was substituted. Also, I was required to
place single quotes around the state. I could have written line six
as *author_state = '&state';*. SQL*Plus defaults to VERIFY=ON
which is why it shows you the old and new line. To turn that
feature off set VERIFY=OFF. Each time SQL*Plus encounters
the *&state* variable, it will ask for input. If you use the variable
more than once, use the && for each occurrence. That tells
SQL*Plus to reuse the already entered variable, or if one has not
been entered, ask for it.

You can also define a variable in the script using the DEFINE
command.

```
SQL> DEFINE state = MO
SQL> SELECT
  2    author_last_name "Last Name"
  3  FROM
  4    author
  5  WHERE
  6    author_state = '&state';
old    6:    author_state = '&state'
new    6:    author_state = 'MO'

Last Name
----------------------------------------
jones
hester
weaton
```

Here, I defined the state at the beginning of my script and
SQL*Plus simply substituted it as the query executed. The
DEFINE command set the variable, and it stays set until you set
DEFINE OFF or you exit SQL*Plus.

Restricting SQL Output

So far, our SQL queries have returned all the rows in the table. As your tables grow large, this becomes a problem. In this section, we will discuss reducing the rows returned to just the ones we want.

The Distinct Clause

Many times there are multiple rows with the same value, and we want to return only one copy of the row. If the boss wants a list of the states where the authors live, we can query that from the AUTHOR table.

```
SQL> SELECT
  2     author_state
  3  FROM
  4     author;

AU
--
MO
MO
MO
CA
IL
TX
WI
KY
LA
MA

10 rows selected.
```

We have ten authors, and we got ten rows back. But, notice that some authors live in the same state. What we want is a list of distinct stats (one row for each state). SQL provides the DISTINCT clause for this result.

```
SQL> SELECT
  2     DISTINCT (author_state)
  3  FROM
  4     author;
```

```
AU
--
CA
IL
KY
LA
MA
MO
TX
WI

8 rows selected.
```

The DISTINCT clause removed the duplicate rows.

The WHERE Clause

The WHERE clause also limits the number of rows in the results set. The WHERE clause is a logical comparison and returns the row if the WHERE clause is true and excludes the row is the clause is false. To list the author last name of those authors that live in MO, use the clause: WHERE *author_state* = *'MO'*; :

```
SQL> SELECT
  2    author_last_name
  3  FROM
  4    author
  5  WHERE author_state = 'MO';

AUTHOR_LAST_NAME
-----------------------------------------
jones
hester
weaton
```

Notice that the column used in the WHERE clause is not one of my selected columns. It can be, but there is no requirement for it to be selected. Also, note that I capitalized the state (MO). The *author_state* column is a *varchar2* or a character string. Character strings are enclosed in single quotes. Although capitalization does not matter in the SQL command syntax, it does matter with data. The state is stored in the database as MO. If I query 'mo' or 'Mo,' I would get no rows returned. In the comparison, the database is making exact comparisons. In chapter 2, we discuss functions that allow you to query data if you do not know how it is stored.

Dates and SQL

Dates are stored in the database as large numbers. The actual size of the data number is dependent on the operating system supporting the database. When a date is requested, it is returned in a human readable form.

When date values are compared in the WHERE clause, the format of the date must match the format that the database is using or the comparison will fail. Alternately, if you are using another format, then you must tell the database how your date is formatted. The default format that the Oracle database uses is: DD-Mon-YY. This is how SQL*Plus will show you the data, when requested. So, how do I reformat the date returned? We will cover date functions in single row functions in Chapter 2.

To get the current date, you select from a function called SYSDATE. SYSDATE returns the current date from the server operating system supporting the database.

```
SQL> SELECT SYSDATE FROM dual;

SYSDATE
---------
23-JAN-05
```

The dual table is a pseudo-table that allows you to execute functions that require selecting from a table.

Lastly, because a date is stored in the database as a number, you can perform date math.

```
SQL> SELECT
  2      SYSDATE Today,
  3      SYSDATE - 1 Yesterday,
  4      SYSDATE + 1 Tomorrow
  5  FROM
  6      dual;

TODAY      YESTERDAY TOMORROW
---------  --------- ---------
23-JAN-05  22-JAN-05 24-JAN-05
```

As you can see, the standard unit in date math is one day. When you add time to the date with SQL updates, you do it in fractions of a day.

```
1 Day      1             1          1
1 Hour     1/24          1/24       0.0417
1 Min      1/(24x60)     1/1440     .000694
1 Sec      1/(24x60x60)  1/86400    .000011574
```

The notation in the second column is most commonly used, because it is so much easier to read. Five minutes is 5/(24x60), much easier than 5/1440 or .00347. When we get to date functions in Chapter 2, you will see that there are functions to do date math by months, weeks and so forth.

Using SQL Comparison Operators

A comparison operator evaluates two values and returns a TRUE, FALSE or NULL. Comparison operates are used in the WHERE clause to limit the number of returned rows.

Equals	=	WHERE first_name = 'BILL'
Not Equals	!=	WHERE state != 'FL'
	<>	WHERE state <> 'FL'
	^=	WHERE state ^= 'FL'
Less Than	<	WHERE pay < min_wage
Greater Than	>	WHERE pay > my_pay
Less Than or Equal	<=	WHERE pay <= 2000
Greater Than or Equal	>=	WHERE pay >= 100000

There are special comparison operators that are used with multiple values.

- **Between...and...** Validates that a value is between the first and second values, inclusive. WHERE *pay* between 100000 and 150000

- **IN (...)** Validates that a value is contained in the list of values. WHERE state IN ('FL', 'CO', 'UT', 'GA')

- **LIKE** Like matches a character pattern. There are two special characters used to match characters. The percent % is zero or more characters wildcard (like the OS * character). The underscore _ is a single character wild card. WHERE name LIKE 'sam%' will return any match that starts with 'sam', including the word sam. (sam, sammy, samatha, samer, etc). If you are looking to match one of the special characters, you must include an escape character so that the database treats it for what it is and not as a wildcard character. For example, if I wanted to get all the rows where *process_name* started with *ora_* , I would have to escape the _ character. WHERE *process_name* LIKE 'ora_%'.

- **NOT** The NOT operator simply negates the operator following. NOT IN, NOT BETWEEN, NOT LIKE.

- **ANY, SOME, ALL** These operators follow an =, !=, <,>,<= or >= operator. They allow these normally single values comparison operators to work with multiple values in a list or returned by a subquery.

- **ANY** Returns TRUE if any value in the list satisfies the operator. The SOME operator is interchangeable with the ANY operator. WHERE *state* = ANY (select *author_state* from AUTHOR)

- **ALL** Returns TRUE only if all values in the list satisfy the comparison. WHERE *pay* < ALL (100000, 150000, 200000).

pay of 80000 will return TRUE, but *pay* of 125000 will return FALSE.

- **EXIST** The EXIST operator returns TRUE if a subquery returns at least one row. Likewise, NOT EXIST returns TRUE if the subquery does not return at least one row.

- **IS NULL** Returns TRUE if the value is NULL. IS NOT NULL returns TRUE if the value is not NULL. WHERE *author_state* IS NULL.

SQL Logical Operators

A SQL query can only have one WHERE clause; however, that clause can contain multiple comparisons. Each comparison returns a TRUE, FALSE or NULL. You evaluate these TRUE/FALSE results using AND and OR to end up with the single TRUE or FALSE for the entire WHERE clause. The AND operator (called conjunction) returns TRUE if both comparisons are TRUE and returns FALSE if either comparison is FALSE.

```
WHERE salary < 100000     -- TRUE
AND  dept = 'SALES'       -- TRUE
```

Since both comparisons are TRUE, the WHERE clause is TRUE. The logical OR operator (called a disjunction) returns TRUE if either comparison is TRUE , otherwise returns FALSE.

```
WHERE salary < 100000     -- TRUE
OR  dept = 'SALES'        -- FALSE
```

The WHERE clause returns TRUE.

Order of Precedence in SQL

It is important to understand how the database evaluates multiple comparisons in the WHERE clause. All the AND comparisons (evaluated from Left to Right) are evaluated before the OR comparisons (evaluated from Left to Right). For example:

```
SELECT
   Last_name,
   Dept,
   Salary
FROM
   employee
WHERE
   dept = 'FINANCE'
OR
   dept = 'SALES'
AND
   salary < 100000;
```

As you read this query, it appears that you collect all the employees from the finance and sales department and then check that the salary is less than 1000000. In this case, you would be wrong! The database will evaluate the AND before the OR. What this query actually does is list employees in SALES with salary < 100000, and all the employees in the FINANCE department.

The database will evaluate all ANDs then all ORs from left to right.

Conclusion

This chapter has covered a lot of ground. Starting with Entity Relationship diagrams, we move to a brief discussion of how Oracle executes an SQL statement, and finally covered the basic SELECT statement and the comparison and logical operators.

A database is any program that stores data and allows you to retrieve that data. When you begin designing your database, it is best to start with a generalized Entity Relation Diagram. By developing the ERD, you will begin to see how the data relates, what the main Entities are and how they relate to each other. Once you have your basis ERD, you can begin the normalization process. During normalization, your goal is to remove redundancy and unrelated data to their own tables.

Next, we introduced the Oracle database and how it goes about retrieving the data you request. All data is manipulated in the buffer cache. By normalizing your data, you end up retrieving less data to get your answer and make better use of the buffer cache. The library cache is used to store SQL and their execution plans. If a SQL statement is re-executed, the execution plan can quickly be reused from the library cache. The *log_buffer* and the undo logs store data changes. They used to provide Oracle's consistent view. In an Oracle database, no one can see uncommitted data changes except the person that made the change.

Finally, we introduced the basic SELECT statement. We demonstrated how to find what columns are in a table using the describe command (*desc*). We introduced the three views *user/all/dba* and how to use them. After talking about SQL*Plus, we covered the options to reformat the output into readable, professional output. Formatting output will be a constant theme throughout the book. Finally, we introduced SQL's comparison and logical operators. These operators are critical to unsure that your queries return the information you are looking for.

In the next chapter, we will introduce Oracle's data types, single, multi-row and date functions.

SQL Functions

SQL Functions

In this chapter, we are going to introduce Oracle's data types. This defines the set of data that can be stored in the Oracle database. Next, we will introduce Oracle functions, starting with single row functions, date functions and progressing through multi-row functions. Oracle functions provide an extraordinary capability to manipulate data as it is queried and returned.

But first, we need to discuss Oracle data types. Oracle has three basic data types; numbers, characters (or strings), and dates. Each data type has a different set of functions for manipulation and conversion.

Oracle Data Types

SQL has several standard data types, and we need to match the data types when we start writing SQL. In this section, we will introduce the set of data types that are part of the Oracle database. These data types are called basic or built-in data types. As we will see near the end of this section, you can use these basic data type to create your own data types.

When you create a table, you must define a data type for each column in that table. For example, here we define a table with a variable character data type (VARCHAR), a date data type and a number data type:

```
create table customer
(
   customer_name     varchar(50),
   birth_date        date,
   income            number
);
```

The basic Oracle data types fall into the following categories: character; number; date; LOBs; and RAW. The two main character data types are the char and the varchar2.

char

The char data type defines a fixed length character string. This string is a list of characters and can be zero or more characters long. A char data type is stored in the database as the size it was created. If I have a table column called *first_name* and I define it as a char(30), I can store any name in that column as long as it does not exceed 30 characters. If I store 'Sam' in that column, Oracle will pad Sam with spaces to fill the 30 characters.

Currently, Oracle limits the size of a char data type to 2000 characters (char(2000)). When the database compares a char data type, the trailing spaces are ignored.

varchar2

The varchar2 is the most common and flexible character data type. The varchar2 is similar to the char except it does not pad the data with spaces. If I create a column called *last_name* as a varchar2(60), and I load the name "Thumb", only five character spaces are used. If I later modify the data to "Thumbbanger," the field in the database will grow to hold the larger name.

The advantage is that space is not wasted in the database filling the field with spaces. If I create a varchar2(60) and a varchar2(1000) and place 'Sam' in both, they will take up the same amount of space in the database.

The maximum size of a varchar2 in a table column is 4000 characters. So, why not make all my character columns varchar2(4000)s? Because you don't want that much data in each of those fields. You would have to insure that your application could handle a returning 4000 byte field. This would quickly become problematic.

Because the database does not pad the field with spaces, it assumes that a space at the end of the field was placed there on purpose and includes it in any comparison operation ("Bob" < "Bob ").

Note that varchar and varchar2 are synonyms. However, varchar has been depreciated and may be removed from future versions, so you should not use it.

nchar and nvarchar2

National character set strings. Both of these are char and varchar2 data types support native languages of the users. These are used if we have to support multi-byte character sets like Chinese Kanji.

long

The long data type is depreciated and may not be available in future releases. You should not use Long data types. It is a bigger version of a varchar2 that could hold up to 2 Gigabytes.

number(p,s)

A number data type is very versatile. In most languages, you must define the precision of a number by declaring it as an integer, double, flout, etc. In the Oracle database, all of these types are incorporated into the number data type. It stores zero, positive, negative, fixed or floating-point numbers. Precision can range from one to 38. Scale can range from –84 to 127. Oracle numbers can sometimes be confusing. The database stores the number as entered. Precision and scale settings do not affect how the number is stored in the database; however, if you exceed the defined precision the database will return a numeric error. This can lead to cases where a value returned has some of its fractional part rounded (scale too small), but when that field is used in an equation, the fractional part is still there.

Remember, defining the precision and scale are optional.

The ANSI numbered data types are supported; however, they are mapped to a number data type. For example, if you create a column as an INTEGER (an ANSI data type), the database would create it as a number(38).

date

The date data type was introduced in the last chapter. It stores date and time as an internal number and can store a date up to a one-second time precision. However, if you try to use a date data type to time events, you cannot capture the fractional second data. In SQL*Plus and some applications, you insert a date by converting the character representation into the date using a function called *to_date*. Some languages (Java for instance) can pass a date object directly into the database with having to convert it.

timestamp(p)

The timestamp data type was introduced in Oracle9i. It functions similarly to the date data type, except that it maintains fractional seconds to a precision from zero to nine, with the default being six. The timestamp data type is only used when fractional seconds are needed, such as records of very small units of time like milliseconds.

Large Objects (*LOB*)

People are putting more and more non-test stuff in their databases. When they start placing pictures, video files, even their MS Word documents into the database, the database has to have a way to handle this unstructured data. Enter the Large Object (LOB) data type. A LOB stores unstructured data as an object. It is stored offline, which means that a reference is stored in the table and the actual object is stored somewhere else. This is important because a LOB can contain up to 4 Gigabytes of data. Imagine searching a table with four LOB columns and a million rows if the LOBs were stored in the table columns! LOBs come in 4 types.

- CLOB – Character LOB
- BLOB – Binary LOB
- NCLOB – National Language CLOB
- BFILE – File Stored outside the database on the server.

You manipulate LOBs using the *dbms_lob* package.

raw

A raw data type is data that is treated as binary data in that there is not manipulation by the database. It is inserted as received and retrieved as is. No character set conversion, etc. A raw data type can be up to 2000 bytes in length.

longraw

Like the long data type, the longraw has been depreciated and should not be used.

---

rowid

A rowid is a hexadecimal string representing the unique address of a row in its table. You cannot store the logical rowid of an index-organized table.

urowid

Universal rowid. Same as rowid except that it can store both physical and logical rowids, including those from an index-organized table. Can also store a foreign table rowed, including those from remote non-oracle databases.

So these are the Oracle basic data types. Oracle allows you to create your own data types, but they must be constructed from the basic data types. For example, if I wanted to have a column that contained the complete author address, I could create my own data type.

```
CREATE OR REPLACE TYPE  full_mailing_address_type
AS OBJECT
( Street        VARCHAR2(80),
  City          VARCHAR2(80),
  State         CHAR(2),
  Zip           VARCHAR2(10) );
```

Here, I created a type called *full_mailing_address_type*. I defined it using the Oracle built-in data types. Once I have created this type in the database, I can use it in a table column. This is called a user defined data type.

```
CREATE TABLE customer
   (
    full_name           full_name_type,
    full_address        full_mailing_address_type,
   );
```

Here, I created a table with two columns, each containing a user defined data type. The *full_address* column contains all the fields of my *full_mailing_address_type* data type. User defined data types are a powerful feature but a bit advanced for this book, so we will confine our examples to the Oracle built-in data types.

Built-in SQL Functions

Basically a function takes one or more inputs and returns one value as a result. All programming languages support functions, and the Oracle database uses a language called PL/SQL to supply most of the standard functions.

Once you learn PL/SQL, you can write your own functions, but here we will stick with the functions that are supplied with the Oracle database. In SQL, a function works on one or more rows of data and returns a result. If a function only works with one row, it is called a single row function. Its counterpart, the multi-row function, takes one or more rows and returns one value. We are going to start with the single-row character function.

A single row function acts on only one row and returns only one result per row. Let's start with character functions.

Character or Text Functions

Character functions are used to modify a char or varchar2 column. We may need to modify the column before comparing it to another value, or we may need it in a different format that it is stored in the database. Sometimes we do not know how he characters are stored, so we use a character function to insure that it is formatted the way we need it.

upper(...)/lower(...)/initcap (...)

Both the *upper* and *lower* function accepts a character string and converts all the character either to upper case or lower case.

```
SQL> SELECT
  2    author_last_name
  3  FROM
  4    author;

AUTHOR_LAST_NAME
----------------------------------------
jones
hester
weaton
jeckle
withers
petty
clark
mee
shagger
smith

10 rows selected.

SQL> SELECT
  2    UPPER(author_last_name) Name
  3  FROM
  4    author;

NAME
----------------------------------------
JONES
HESTER
WEATON
JECKLE
WITHERS
PETTY
CLARK
MEE
SHAGGER
SMITH

10 rows selected.
```

Another character function is the *initcap* function. As you can guess from the name, it capitalizes only the first character of each word. Let's look at an example of each type. Notice that I formatted my output for easy reading. I set my SQL*Plus parameters, defined my columns. Created my query and then reset my environment. Remember, when you define a column in SQL*Plus, it stays defined and will by applied to any column returning with that name until you CLEAR it or exit SQL*Plus.

```
set pages 999 lines 90 feedback off
column c1 heading Caps    format a20
column c2 heading Lower   format a20
column c3 heading Best    format a20

SELECT
  UPPER(author_last_name)   c1,
  LOWER(author_last_name)   c2,
  INITCAP(author_last_name) c3
FROM
  author;

set lines 70 feedback on
clear columns
```

```
Caps                 Lower                Best
-------------------- -------------------- --------------------
JONES                jones                Jones
HESTER               hester               Hester
WEATON               weaton               Weaton
JECKLE               jeckle               Jeckle
WITHERS              withers              Withers
PETTY                petty                Petty
CLARK                clark                Clark
MEE                  mee                  Mee
SHAGGER              shagger              Shagger
SMITH                smith                Smith
```

In these examples, I am applying the function to a column from the query. However, these functions can be applied to any character input.

```
SELECT
  UPPER('This is an EXAMPLE')   c1,
  LOWER('This is an EXAMPLE')   c2,
  INITCAP('This is an EXAMPLE') c3
FROM
  dual;

Caps                 Lower                Best
-------------------- -------------------- --------------------
THIS IS AN EXAMPLE   this is an example   This Is An Example
```

When we covered comparison operators, I said that capitalization in a SQL query does not matter except for data. For example, if I want to find the author names for all authors that live in St. Louis, I need to correctly provide the data for the equal operator.

```
SQL> SELECT
  2     author_last_name
  3  FROM
  4     author
  5  WHERE
  6     author_city = 'St. Louis';

no rows selected
```

But, I know there are authors that live in St. Louis. It must be
that the case is incorrect. Let's try again.

```
SQL> SELECT
  2     author_last_name
  3  FROM
  4     author
  5  WHERE
  6     UPPER(author_city) = 'ST. LOUIS';

AUTHOR_LAST_NAME
----------------------------------------
jones
hester
weaton

3 rows selected.
```

OK, I found my authors. Now, my boss is always asking for a
list of authors that live in different cities. So, I need to take this
query and make a file that will ask me for a city name and then
list the authors for that city. While we are at it, let's get the whole
name and make it look nice. One thing I have to watch out for is
that some one else may use my script and not know that I am
comparing upper case. Just to make sure, we will upper case the
variable also.

```
-- auth_city.sql
-- Authors from a Specific City
--
set pages 999 lines 90 feedback on

column Name format a20
column City format a15

SELECT
  INITCAP(author_first_name||' '||author_last_name) Name,
  INITCAP(author_city) City
```

```
FROM
  author
WHERE
  UPPER(author_city) = UPPER('&city_name');

set line 70 verify on pages 999
clear columns
-- End


SQL> @auth_city.sql
Enter value for city_name: St. Louis

NAME                 CITY
-------------------- ----------------
Mark Jones           St. Louis
Alvis Hester         St. Louis
Erin Weaton          St. Louis

3 rows selected.
```

Again, I used the *upper* function to change both the input variable *city_name* and the *author_city* in the comparison. I set my SQL*Plus variables, set the columns, ran the query, reset the SQL*Plus variables back to my default and cleared the column definitions.

Notice that I turned *verify* OFF to get rid of the "old and new" lines, but I left *feedback* ON. That way, if my boss asks for authors that live in a city that is not in the database, my report tells me that no rows were returned. This is usually better than a blank report.

Now, when my boss asks for authors from a certain city, all I have to do is start SQL*Plus, execute my script and give the boss the report. We are on our way to that pay raise (we cover updates in the next chapter).

concat (s1, s2)

In the last chapter, we introduced concatenation using the double vertical bars (| |). The *concat* function does the same thing.

concat(s1, s2) is the same as s1||s2 where s1 and s2 are character strings.

```
SQL> SELECT
  2     CONCAT('The author Named ', author_last_name) Name
  3     FROM
  4        author;

NAME
----------------------------------------------------------
The author Named jones
The author Named hester
The author Named weaton
The author Named jeckle
The author Named withers
The author Named petty
The author Named clark
The author Named mee
The author Named shagger
The author Named smith
```

Well, we got what we asked for, but that looks pretty bad. We will never get that raise if we keep sending reports like that to the boss. Lucky for us, you can nest functions.

```
column Name1 format a30
column Name2 format a30

SELECT
   INITCAP(CONCAT('The author Named ', author_last_name)) Name1,
   CONCAT(INITCAP('The author Named '), UPPER(author_last_name))
Name2
   FROM
      author;
clear columns

NAME1                            NAME2
------------------------------   ------------------------------
The Author Named Jones           The Author Named JONES
The Author Named Hester          The Author Named HESTER
The Author Named Weaton          The Author Named WEATON
The Author Named Jeckle          The Author Named JECKLE
The Author Named Withers         The Author Named WITHERS
The Author Named Petty           The Author Named PETTY
The Author Named Clark           The Author Named CLARK
The Author Named Mee             The Author Named MEE
The Author Named Shagger         The Author Named SHAGGER
The Author Named Smith           The Author Named SMITH
```

Notice the parentheses define the order that the functions are evaluated, from inside to outside.

substr (s1, b, n)

The *substr* function is used to extract a portion of a string. It returns the part of s1 that starts at location b and includes n characters.

```
SELECT
  SUBSTR('Now is the time for all good men',1,3)
FROM
  dual;

SUB
---
Now

1 row selected.
```

instr (s1, s2, st, t)

The *instr* function is similar to the *substr*, except instead of returning the sub string, *instr* returns the location of the string. The parameters include s1, the string we are search in, s2, the string we are searching for, st is the character location to start looking, and t, which is the number of the occurrence we are looking for (the fourth occurrence, for instance). Both st and t default to one, which will result in searching for the first occurrence starting at the beginning of the string.

```
SELECT
  INSTR('Now is the time for all good men',' ',1,3)
FROM
  dual;

INSTR('NOWISTHETIMEFORALLGOODMEN','',1,3)
---------------------------------------
                                     11

1 row selected.
```

In the example above, I am looking for the third occurrence of the string " " (a space) starting at the beginning. The third space in the string is at character number 11.

Now for a little challenge. Suppose that my boss wants to know what the first word of every book title is. Don't wonder why, the boss wants it, so we will get it. Think about the solution before looking at the answer below.

```
SELECT
  SUBSTR(book_title,1,(INSTR(book_title,' ',1,1)-1)) "First Word"
FROM
  book;

First Word
------------------------------------------------------------------
windows
piano
DOS
The
zero
operations
non
UNIX
pay
the
writers
managing
bears
reduce
the
oracle9i
was
cooking
never
how

20 rows selected.
```

Basically, I queried a substring of the book title starting at the first character, until the first space, minus one to remove the space from the results. This type of query is actually very common on databases that are not properly normalized. If the author names were stored in our PUBS database in one column, we would have to use this type of query to separate the first and last names when needed.

length(s1)

Sometimes we just need to know how many characters there are in a string. The *length* function returns the length of s1.

```
SELECT
  INITCAP(author_last_name)  Name,
  LENGTH(author_last_name)   Sz
FROM
  author;

NAME                         SZ
-------------------- ----------
Jones                         5
Hester                        6
Weaton                        6
Jeckle                        6
Withers                       7
Petty                         5
Clark                         5
Mcc                           3
Shagger                       7
Smith                         5
```

lpad (s1, s, c)/rpad (s1, s, c)

When you want to pad a string, you use *lpad* and *rpad*. *Lpad* pads the string s1 until it is the size s using the character c by adding character c to the left side of s1. *Rpad* does the same thing but adds the character c to the right side.

```
SELECT
  LPAD('Hello',10,'*')  Left,
  RPAD('Hello',10,'*')  Right,
  LPAD('Hello',10)      LSpace,
  RPAD('Hello ',10,'-') Dashes
from dual;

LEFT       RIGHT      LSPACE     DASHES
---------- ---------- ---------- ----------
*****Hello Hello*****      Hello Hello ----

1 row selected.
```

That crazy boss (in my case, Don Burleson) is at it again. Now he wants to know the length of the author's names. Since it is going to the boss, we want it to look nice along with being accurate. The author's name is first name, a space, and last name. As the boss's requests get more complicated (and strange), we need a method to insure that the data we provide him is correct. I have always found it easier to focus on the data first, then the formatting. Lastly, don't waste the effort; place it in a script so you can use it again.

First, let's get the data.

```
SELECT
  INITCAP(author_first_name||' '||author_last_name),
  LENGTH(author_first_name||' '||author_last_name)
FROM
  author;

INITCAP(AUTHOR_FIRST_NAME||''||AUTHOR_LAST_NAME)
--------------------------------------------------------
LENGTH(AUTHOR_FIRST_NAME||''||AUTHOR_LAST_NAME)
-----------------------------------------------
Mark Jones
                                                      10
Alvis Hester
                                                      12
Erin Weaton
                                                      11
Pierre Jeckle
                                                      13
Lester Withers
                                                      14
Juan Petty
                                                      10
Louis Clark
                                                      11
Minnie Mee
                                                      10
Dirk Shagger
                                                      12
Diego Smith
                                                      11
10 rows selected.
```

Now, let's turn the query into a script and make it pretty for the boss. I want set the author name column to 40 characters wide and use the dot (.) or period to fill out the space to the right using *rpad*.

```
-- auth_name_length.sql
--
column c1 Heading "Author Name" format a40
column c2 Heading Size          format 999

SELECT
  RPAD(INITCAP(author_first_name||' '||author_last_name),40,'.')
c1,
  LENGTH(author_first_name||' '||author_last_name)              c2
FROM
  author;

clear columns

Author Name                              Size
---------------------------------------- ----
Mark Jones.............................    10
Alvis Hester...........................    12
Erin Weaton............................    11
Pierre Jeckle..........................    13
Lester Withers.........................    14
Juan Petty.............................    10
Louis Clark............................    11
Minnie Mee.............................    10
Dirk Shagger...........................    12
Diego Smith............................    11
```

Now we have something that will impress the boss. Maybe that raise is not that far fetched an idea after all!

ltrim (s1, s2)/rtrim (s1, s2)

Sometimes you need to remove characters from the beginning and/or end of a string. Normally you are removing spaces, but you may need to remove other characters. *Ltrim* removes any character in s2 from the front of s1. Think of s2 as a list of characters rather than a word. *Rtrim* does the same thing except it removes the character from the end of s1. The string s2 defaults to a space. If the characters in s2 are not in s1, then s1 is returned unchanged.

trim (s2 from s1)

The *trim* function incorporates both *ltrim* and *rtrim* in one command. You can set trim to remove leading, trailing or both.

The default is both. The string s2 defaults to a space. When using *trim*, you can only define one character to trim. With *rtrim* or *ltrim*, you are not restricted.

```
SELECT
  LTRIM('abcdedcba', 'abc') Left,
  RTRIM('abcdedcba', 'abc') Right,
  TRIM(LEADING 'a' FROM 'abcdedcba') TRIML,
  TRIM(TRAILING 'a' FROM 'abcdedcba') TRIMR,
  TRIM(BOTH 'a' FROM 'abcdedcba') TRIMB
FROM
  dual;

LEFT    RIGHT   TRIML     TRIMR     TRIMB
------  ------  --------  --------  -------
dedcba  abcded  bcdedcba  abcdedcb  bcdedcb

1 row selected.
```

There are a number of other text functions, but they normally apply more to PL/SQL programmers and are rarely used in a SQL query.

Number Functions

Number functions allow you to present a number in a manner that is useful to the reader. You must always be careful with converting numbers because you are only converting the presentation. The number is in the database is still the same.

round (n,d)

The *round* function rounds a number n to the specified decimal d. The decimal d can be positive, negative or zero. If the decimal is positive, then the number is rounded to that many decimal points. The number five rounds up. If d is zero, then the number is rounded to no decimal points. If d is negative, then the number will have no decimal points and it will be rounded to the d digits to the left of the decimal point.

```
SELECT
   ROUND( 1234.345, 2),
   ROUND( 1234.345, 0),
   ROUND( 1234.345, -2)
FROM
   dual;

ROUND(1234.345,2) ROUND(1234.345,0) ROUND(1234.345,-2)
----------------- ----------------- ------------------
          1234.35              1234               1200

1 row selected.
```

The boss now wants to know the retail price of the books we publish, rounded to the nearest dollar. This is found in the book table.

```
SELECT
   RPAD(TRIM(INITCAP(book_title)),40,'.') Title,
   ROUND(book_retail_price,0) Bucks
FROM
   book;


TITLE                                         BUCKS
----------------------------------------- ----------
Windows Success.........................      35
Piano Greats............................      33
Dos For Dummies.........................      20
The Zen Of Auto Repair..................      100
Zero Loss Finance.......................      22
Operations Research Theory..............      45
Non Violins In The Workplace............      12
Unix For Experts........................      39
Pay No Taxes And Go To Jail.............      11
The Fall Of Microsoft...................      20
Writers Market..........................      23
Managing Stress.........................      40
Bears Are People Too....................      35
Reduce Spending The Republican Way......      28
The Willow Weeps No More................      30
Oracle9i Sql Tuning.....................      50
Was George Washington Feeble?...........      25
Cooking Light...........................      25
Never Eat Meat..........................      11
How To Housebreak Your Horse............      30

20 rows selected.
```

trunc (n,d)

The *trunc* or truncate function simply drops the digits without rounding. The decimal d can again be positive, negative or zero. If the number truncated is five or higher, it is still dropped without rounding the next digit up.

```
SELECT
  TRUNC( 1234.345, 2),
  TRUNC( 1234.345, 0),
  TRUNC( 1234.345, -2)
FROM
  dual;


TRUNC(1234.345,2) TRUNC(1234.345,0) TRUNC(1234.345,-2)
----------------- ----------------- ------------------
         1234.34              1234                1200

1 row selected.
```

Notice the difference between *trunc* and *round*.

```
TRUNC(1234.345,2) TRUNC(1234.345,0) TRUNC(1234.345,-2)
----------------- ----------------- ------------------
         1234.34              1234                1200

ROUND(1234.345,2) ROUND(1234.345,0) ROUND(1234.345,-2)
----------------- ----------------- ------------------
         1234.35              1234                1200
```

Like the character functions, there are more numeric functions that are mostly used by programmers such as *sin, cos, tan, ceil, floor,* etc.

Date Functions

Dates are stored in the database as a number that contains both the calendar data information and the time information. We already discussed date math, where the unit of measure is one day. Date functions allow you to modify and compare date data types. Dates can be tricky. If you use SYSDATE to insert date columns in tables, you will not only get the date component but also the time component.

If you want to see all the records from today, a query based on today's date will not match any rows in the database. Basically, the times components of the two dates will not match. This section will explain how to work with date data types and the next section will explain converting characters to dates and back again. When working with calendars, you also have the problem that all months do not have the same number of days in them. If you have a date and want the same date in three months, it becomes problematic.

months_between (l,e)

This function returns the months between two dates. If I wanted to know how many months an employee has worked for the company, I can use this function. There is an *emp_hire_date* in the emp table.

```
SELECT
  MONTHS_BETWEEN(SYSDATE,EMP_DATE_OF_HIRE)
FROM
  emp;

MONTHS_BETWEEN(SYSDATE,EMP_DATE_OF_HIRE)
----------------------------------------
                              58.7710805
                              70.7710805
                              34.7710805
                              46.7710805
                              34.7710805
                              82.7710805
                              106.77108
                              154.77108
                              178.77108
                              166.77108
10 rows selected.
```

Notice that it returns the fraction of a month. You could use *trunc* or *round* to make the results more readable.

add_months (d,n)

The *add_months* function gives you the same day, n number of months away. The n can be positive or negative.

```
SELECT
  SYSDATE,
  ADD_MONTHS(SYSDATE,1),
  ADD_MONTHS(SYSDATE,2),
  ADD_MONTHS(SYSDATE,3),
  ADD_MONTHS(SYSDATE,4),
  ADD_MONTHS(SYSDATE,5),
  ADD_MONTHS(SYSDATE,6)
FROM
  dual;

SYSDATE    ADD_MONTH ADD_MONTH ADD_MONTH ADD_MONTH ADD_MONTH ADD_MONTH
--------- --------- --------- --------- --------- --------- ---------
24-JAN-05 24-FEB-05 24-MAR-05 24-APR-05 24-MAY-05 24-JUN-05 24-JUL-05

SELECT
  SYSDATE,
  ADD_MONTHS(SYSDATE,-1),
  ADD_MONTHS(SYSDATE,-2),
  ADD_MONTHS(SYSDATE,-3),
  ADD_MONTHS(SYSDATE,-4),
  ADD_MONTHS(SYSDATE,-5),
  ADD_MONTHS(SYSDATE,-6)
FROM
  dual;

SYSDATE    ADD_MONTH ADD_MONTH ADD_MONTH ADD_MONTH ADD_MONTH ADD_MONTH
--------- --------- --------- --------- --------- --------- ---------
24-JAN-05 24-DEC-04 24-NOV-04 24-OCT-04 24-SEP-04 24-AUG-04 24-JUL-04
```

last_day (d)

The *last_day* function returns the last day of the month of the date d. If you want to find the first day of the next month, simply add one to the *last_day* results.

```
SELECT
  SYSDATE,
  LAST_DAY(SYSDATE) EOM,
  LAST_DAY(SYSDATE)+1 FOM
FROM dual;

SYSDATE   EOM       FOM
--------- --------- ---------
24-JAN-05 31-JAN-05 01-FEB-05
```

next_day (d, day_of_week)

The *next_day* function returns the date of the *day_of_week* after date d. *day_of_week* can be the full name or abbreviation. Below, we get the date for next Monday, next Friday, and the first Tuesday of next month.

```
SELECT
  SYSDATE,
  NEXT_DAY(SYSDATE,'MONDAY')  "Next Mon",
  NEXT_DAY(SYSDATE,'FRIDAY')  "Next Fri",
  NEXT_DAY(LAST_DAY(SYSDATE)+1,'TUESDAY')  "First Tue"
FROM dual;


SYSDATE    Next Mon  Next Fri  First Tue
---------  --------- --------- ---------
24-JAN-05  31-JAN-05 28-JAN-05 08-FEB-05
```

round (d, format)

We talked about the *round* function as a numeric function but it is also a date function. The *round* function returns the date rounded to the format.

```
SELECT
  SYSDATE,
  ROUND(SYSDATE,'MONTH')  Month,
  ROUND(SYSDATE,'YEAR')   Year
FROM
  dual;

SYSDATE    MONTH      YEAR
---------  ---------  ---------
24-JAN-05  01-FEB-05  01-JAN-05
```

Notice that SYSDATE is past midmonth so the month was rounded to the next month. We are not past midyear, however, so the year was rounded to the beginning of the current year.

---

trunc (d, format)

As with the numeric *trunc*, the date version simply truncates the date to the level specified in the format.

```
SELECT
  SYSDATE,
  TRUNC(SYSDATE,'MONTH') Month,
  TRUNC(SYSDATE,'YEAR')  Year
FROM
  dual;
SYSDATE   MONTH     YEAR
--------- --------- ---------
24-JAN-05 01-JAN-05 01-JAN-05
```

Conversion Functions

Conversion functions change data from on data type to another. Again, there are a significant number of conversion functions; however, most are used primarily in PL/SQL programming. We will focus our attention on the functions most used in SQL queries.

Oracle will do a lot of conversion internally. During assignment, the database will change a varchar2 or char type into a number or date type. Likewise, the database will convert a number or date into a varchar2. During evaluation, the database will only convert varchar2 and char to number and date.

What we want to cover in this section is explicitly converting between numbers, characters and dates. You will see that there are a large number of formatting options. This ability to format the conversion not only allows you great flexibility, but also is key in allowing you to import data from other sources that may be saved in different formats.

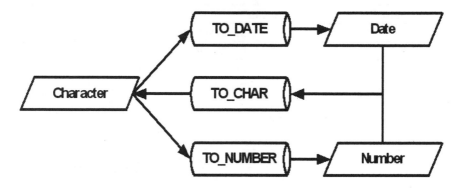

Figure 2.1: *Type Conversions*

In Figure 2.1, we can see the three main conversion function. *to_date* converts characters to dates while *to_number* converts characters to numbers. The *to_char* function takes either a date or a number and converts it to characters. Let's start with the *to_char* function converting dates.

to_char (date, format)

The *to_char* functions will change a date to characters in the format defined in the format field. If you do not define a format, the date will be returned in the default format set for the database.

```
SELECT
  TO_CHAR(SYSDATE)
FROM
  dual;
TO_CHAR(S
---------
25-JAN-05
```

Formatting commands are enclosed in single quotes and are case sensitive and can include any valid date format element.

Element	Format
D	Day of the Week as in 1 thru 7.
DD	Day of the Month as in 1 thru 31.
DDD	Day of the Year as in 1 thru 366.
DY	Day of the Week Abbreviated Mon thru Sun
DAY	Day of the Week Monday, Tuesday…
J	Julian Date. Number of days since 4712 BC.
W	Week of the Month as in 1 thru 5.
WW	Week of the Year as in 1 thru 53.
MM	Month (two digits) as in 01 thru 31.
MON	Month Abbreviated Jan thru Dec.
MONTH	Month Spelled out. January thru December.
YY	Year, last two digits as in 04 and 05.
YYYY	Year, four digit as in 2004 and 2005.
YEAR	Year spelled out.
RR	Year in 2 digits converted as per Y2K Rules.
HH	Hour in 12 hour clock. 1 thru 12.
HH24	Hour in 24 hour clock 1 thru 24.
MI	Minutes as in 1 thru 59.
SS	Seconds as in 1 thru 59.
SSSSS	Seconds of the day as in 1 thr 86399.
AM, PM	Meridian Indicator
A.M., P.M.	Meridian Indicator with periods.

Table 2.1: *Date elements and associated formats*

Let's see some examples to clarify all these formatting command.

```
SELECT
  TO_CHAR(SYSDATE) ,
  TO_CHAR(SYSDATE,'MON-DD-YYYY'),
  TO_CHAR(SYSDATE,'MON:DAY:YYYY'),
  TO_CHAR(SYSDATE,'MONTH, DAY, YEAR')
FROM
  dual;

TO_CHAR(S TO_CHAR(SYS TO_CHAR(SYSDATE,'M
TO_CHAR(SYSDATE,'MONTH,DAY,YEAR')
--------- ----------- ------------------ ------------------------------------
25-JAN-05 JAN-25-2005 JAN:TUESDAY  :2005 JANUARY, TUESDAY  , TWO THOUSAND FIVE
```

First, I retrieved the database default. I then changed the order and format. Notice that I used literal text between the formatting commands. I used a dash (-) on one example and a colon (:) on the other. Lastly, I wrote the entire date out long hand. Next, let's look at the time component of the date.

```
SELECT
  TO_CHAR(SYSDATE) ,
  TO_CHAR(SYSDATE,'HH24'),
  TO_CHAR(SYSDATE,'HH AM'),
  TO_CHAR(SYSDATE,'HH:MM:SS AM')
FROM
  dual;

TO_CHAR(S TO TO_CH TO_CHAR(SYS
--------- -- ----- -----------
25-JAN-05 10 10 AM 10:01:06 AM
```

Again, I first retrieved the database default, which shows no time element at all. I then selected the hour in 24-hour format, the hour in 12-hour format, and lastly the hours, minutes and seconds.

Let's put this to work. In the PUBS schema, there is a table called sales that contains order number and order dates. Let's retrieve the order numbers and the order dates in a format that shows the data and hour the order was placed.

First, describe the sales table.

```
SQL> desc sales
 Name                   Null?    Type
 ---------------------- -------- ----------------------
 STORE_KEY                       VARCHAR2(4)
 BOOK_KEY                        VARCHAR2(6)
 ORDER_NUMBER                    VARCHAR2(20)
 ORDER_DATE                      DATE
 QUANTITY                        NUMBER(5)
```

Next retrieve the *order_number* and the *order_date*.

```
SELECT
  order_number,
  order_date
FROM
  sales;
ORDER_NUMBER          ORDER_DAT
-------------------- ---------
O101                  02-JAN-02
O102                  02-JAN-02
O103                  02-JAN-02
O104                  03-JAN-02
O105                  03-JAN-02
O106                  03-JAN-02
O107                  04-JAN-02
O108                  04-JAN-02
-----------
O198                  19-MAY-02
O199                  20-MAY-02
O200                  21-MAY-02

100 rows selected.
```

Finally, add the formatting with the *to_char* function.

```
SELECT
  order_number "Order",
  TO_CHAR(order_date,'DD-MON-YYYY HH24') "Date"
FROM
  sales;

Order                 Date
-------------------- --------------
O101                  02-JAN-2004 14
O102                  02-JAN-2004 13
O103                  02-JAN-2004 16
O104                  03-JAN-2004 08
O105                  03-JAN-2004 13
O106                  03-JAN-2004 14
O107                  04-JAN-2004 14
O108                  04-JAN-2004 09
O109                  04-JAN-2004 14
O110                  04-JAN-2004 10
O111                  04-JAN-2004 14
O112                  05-JAN-2004 15
O113                  05-JAN-2004 14
O114                  05-JAN-2004 16
O115                  07-JAN-2004 17
O116                  10-FEB-2004 13
O117                  10-FEB-2004 12
O118                  10-FEB-2004 08
O119                  10-FEB-2004 14
O120                  10-FEB-2004 08
O121                  10-FEB-2004 12
O122                  11-FEB-2004 09
```

Notice that I placed the order and date aliases into double quotes. I did that because both are Oracle key words and if I did not quote them, they would confuse the SQL parser.

Now let's put this to use in the comparison operator. Find all the order numbers that were placed at 2 PM (14).

```
SELECT
  order_number "Order"
FROM
  sales
WHERE
  TO_CHAR(order_date,'HH24') = '14';

Order
-------------------
0101
0106
0107
0109
0111
0113
0119
0124
0129
0134
0141
0147
0151
0157
0160
0166
0172
0180
0186
0190

20 rows selected.
```

If I did not place single quotes around the 14 in the where clause, the query would still work. That is because the database would implicitly convert the character hour to a number to compare with the number 14. You would have two conversions, one implicitly (the character to number) and on explicitly (the date to character).

to_char (num, format)

The *to_char* function also converts number to character including formatting. Below is a list of some of the number formatting codes.

Element	Format
9	If digit is present, print it, otherwise blank.
?	If digit is present, print it, otherwise print a 0.
. (Period)	Decimal Point location.
, (Comma)	Comma locations
$	Places $ before number.
S	Places +/- before number to indicate positive or negative number

Table 2.2: *Number elements and associated formats*

This is actually the same as the SQL*Plus Column formatting for a number.

```
SELECT
  TO_CHAR(123456.123456) Ex1,
  TO_CHAR(123456.123456,'999999.99') Ex2,
  TO_CHAR(123456.123456,'$999999.00') Ex3,
  TO_CHAR(123456.123456,'99999.9999') Ex4,
  TO_CHAR(123456.123456,'9,999,999,999.000999') Ex5
FROM
  dual;

EX1            EX2         EX3         EX4          EX5
-------------- ----------  ----------- -----------  -------------------
123456B123456  123456.12  .$123456.12 ##########       123,456.123456
```

Notice that *to_char* rounds the number if there are no sufficient digits behind the decimal point. In example four, there are not enough digits in front of the decimal point, so *to_char* cannot *round* and cannot show the actual number; therefore, it displays the pound signs (#) to indicate that it has a number that can not be displayed in the required format. Also, as you can see in example five, if there is a nine in the format but no digit to

display, the database returns spaces. We can also place leading
zeros if we want.

```
SELECT
  TO_CHAR(123456.123456,'9,999,999,999.000999') Ex5,
  TO_CHAR(123456.123456,'0,000,000,000.00000000') Ex6
FROM
  dual;

EX5                    EX6
-------------------    ------------------------
      123,456.123456   0,000,123,456.12345600
```

Now, let's format the *book_retail_price* from the book table.

```
SELECT
  book_retail_price Ugly,
  TO_CHAR(book_retail_price,'$9,999.00') Pretty
FROM
  book;

UGLY                               PRETTY
--------------------------------   ----------
34B95                                 $34.95
32B95                                 $32.95
19B95                                 $19.95
99B95                                 $99.95
21B95                                 $21.95
44B95                                 $44.95
11B95                                 $11.95
38B95                                 $38.95
10B95                                 $10.95
19B95                                 $19.95
22B95                                 $22.95
39B95                                 $39.95
34B95                                 $34.95
27B95                                 $27.95
29B95                                 $29.95
49B95                                 $49.95
24B95                                 $24.95
24B95                                 $24.95
10B95                                 $10.95
29B95                                 $29.95

20 rows selected.
```

to_date (text, format)

The *to_date* function takes text and uses the formatting codes to
convert the text into a date data type. The format is telling the

---

database that the text is in that format. Remember that the database stores a date as a number, so it must understand what the text is representing as part of that date. The format codes listed in the *to_char* table are the same for the *to_date*. We will use to_date when we start inserting data into our database, but here are a few examples.

TO_DATE('05-05-2004 8:30','MM-DD-YYYY HH24:MI')

```
SELECT
   TO_DATE('25-05-2004 8:30','DD-MM-YYYY HH24:MI')
 FROM
   dual;
TO_DATE('
---------
25-MAY-04
```

The example above takes text and changes it into a date, which is then returned in the database default format.

to_number (text, format)

The *to_number* function takes text and converts it into a number. This function is not used much because the database does this automatically. It only needs to be used to remove formatting

```
SELECT
  12345,
  1,2345
FROM
  dual;


     12345          1       2345
---------- ---------- ----------
     12345          1       2345
```

Here, the database is automatically converting the text to number. Notice that the formatting confused the SQL parser into thinking that the second number was actually two numbers. If I tried it with $12345.00, I would get an ORA-00911: invalid character error on the dollar sign.

nvl (e1,e2)

As we have already discussed, NULL become a problem when evaluating comparisons and in math. The *nvl* function provides a way to work with NULL values. The *nvl* function work with dates, numbers or characters, but both expressions must be the same data type. The *nvl* function will return expression one if it is not NULL. If expression one is NULL, then it returns expression two.

```
if (e1 != NULL) return e1;
else return e2;
```

For example, if an employee's annual salary equaled his monthly pay * 12 + his commission, then we could compute every employee's annual pay with the query below.

```
SELECT
  emp_last_name Name,
  (emp_salary*12)+comm Annual
FROM
  emp;
```

However, any employee that does not get a commission, say an accountant or a secretary, their annual pay would be NULL. Why, because we added a NULL to their salary*12. But, we can use the *nvl* function to get around this problem.

```
SELECT
  emp_last_name Name,
  (emp_salary*12)+NLV(comm,0) Annual
FROM
  emp;
```

Here, if the employee gets a commission the function returns comm, otherwise it returns a zero.

decode

The *decode* function is used to change values. It is used in the same way a case or switch function is used in other programming languages. In fact, Oracle has introduced the case statement, and we will cover that below. You will normally want to use the case function over the decode function.

```
SELECT
  emp_last_name Name,
  emp_salary    Salary,
  DECODE(JOB_KEY, '100','Salsperson',
                  '200','Marketer',
                  '300','Editor',
                  '400','Manager') Job
FROM
  emp;

NAME                                SALARY JOB
------------------------------- ---------- ----------
king                                 95000 Salsperson
jackson                              35000 Salsperson
korn                                 28000 Marketer
linus                                45000 Marketer
tokheim                              63000 Editor
levender                             14000 Editor
johnson                              31000 Editor
baker                                51000 Manager
coleman                              73000 Manager
brannigan                            66666 Manager
```

When it comes to the *decode* function, formatting is the key to success. The decode line in the example above is the same as the one below.

```
DECODE(JOB_KEY,'100','Salsperson','200','Marketer','300','Editor','4
00',-'Manager') Job
```

As you can see, anything but a trivial replacement will become quite difficult to debug or understand. One other problem with *decode* is it is an Oracle specific extension to SQL.

---

case

The *case* function is the ANSI version of *decode*. If performs the same function but has syntax much like a programming language's version of case. It uses the syntax:

```
CASE selection WHEN x THEN y WHEN q THEN r ELSE z END

SELECT
  emp_last_name Name,
  emp_salary    Salary,
  CASE JOB_KEY
    WHEN 100 THEN 'Salsperson'
    WHEN 200 THEN 'Marketer'
    WHEN 300 THEN 'Editor'
    ELSE 'Manager'
    END Job
FROM
  emp;


NAME                            SALARY JOB
------------------------------ ---------- ----------
king                            95000 Salsperson
jackson                         35000 Salsperson
korn                            28000 Marketer
linus                           45000 Marketer
tokheim                         63000 Editor
levender                        14000 Editor
johnson                         31000 Editor
baker                           51000 Manager
coleman                         73000 Manager
brannigan                       66666 Manager

10 rows selected.
```

Notice that there are no commas placed at the end of the when statements. This is all on one line the SQL parser. Also, *job_key* is a number so the evaluation criteria of the when statement must also be a number. However, the case statement in the example above returns a character string.

All of the functions we have discussed so far have been single row functions. They operate on every row returned, but a single row at a time. In the next section, we move into multi row functions, which allow us to aggregate data from multiple rows.

Multi Row SQL Functions

They operate on a set of rows and returns one result or one result per group. We will cover groups in Chapter 3. This is a powerful feature because it allows you to generate subtotals, sums and averages within the SQL that is retrieving the data. For now, we will apply the functions to all the rows we return. In the next chapter, we will break up our returning rows into groups and apply the functions to each of the groups independently.

count

The *count* function counts the number of rows it processes and returns that number. You can use the distinct clause to count only distinct rows.

```
SELECT
  COUNT(*),
  COUNT(1),
  COUNT(store_key),
  COUNT(DISTINCT store_key)
FROM
  sales;
```

COUNT(*)	COUNT(1)	COUNT(STORE_KEY)	COUNT(DISTINCTSTORE_KEY)
100	100	100	10

First, we count the number of rows using *count*(*). In the second example, we do the same thing. Some DBAs believe that *count*(1) is more efficient than *count*(*), but this is a myth. In example three, we count the number of *store_keys*. If a row is processed with a NULL *store_key*, it will be counted in example one and two but not in three or four. In example four, we count distinct *store_keys*. So there are 100 rows in the sales table, each row has a *store_key* (no NULL *store_keys*) and there are ten distinct *store_keys* in the table (listed below).

```
SQL> SELECT DISTINCT store_key FROM sales;

STOR
----
S101
S102
S103
S104
S105
S106
S107
S108
S109
S110
```

sum(c1)

The function *sum* adds the value of the column c1 for all the rows processed and returns the total. NULLs are skipped. *Sum* can also use the distinct format.

```
SELECT
  SUM(quantity)
FROM
  sales;

SUM(QUANTITY)
-------------
       110550

SELECT
  SUM(quantity)
FROM
  sales
WHERE
  book_key = 'B104';

SUM(QUANTITY)
-------------
         4000
```

avg(c1)

The *avg* function returns the average of the column you specify. *Avg* can also use the distinct format. NULLS are skipped, not included as a zero.

```
SELECT
  AVG(quantity)
FROM
  sales;

AVG(QUANTITY)
-------------
      1105.5
```

Below, we get the average of the distinct quantity values in the sales table.

```
SELECT
  AVG(DISTINCT quantity)
FROM
  sales;

AVG(DISTINCTQUANTITY)
---------------------
         2658.46154
```

min(c1)/max(c1)

The *min* and *max* functions returns the smallest and largest values of the column c1. NULLs are skipped. There is no distinct format.

```
SELECT
   MAX(quantity),
   MIN(quantity)
 FROM
   sales
 WHERE
   book_key = 'B105';

MAX(QUANTITY) MIN(QUANTITY)
------------- -------------
          700           100
```

There are other Multi Row Functions such as *stdev* and *variance* that are normally used in PL/SQL.

Conclusion

We covered a lot of information in this chapter. First, we introduced the different Oracle built-in data types. The three most used data types being the character, number and date data types. The varchar2 is the most efficient way to store character data that is not fixed length.

Next, we moved to Single Row Functions. Single row functions operate on every row, one row at a time. These included character functions such as *upper*, *lower* and *initcap*, numeric functions such as *round* and *trunc*, and date functions such as *add_month* etc. It is important to remember that single row functions format the column value but do not change the value stored in the database. When you round a number, it will be displayed in the format that you specify, but if you use the number in an equation before rounding it, the number used in the equation is the entire number stored in the database.

We then discussed single row functions that convert data between characters, dates and numbers. Note that if you format a character and the format does not contain enough digits to display the number, it will be displayed as pound signs (####).

Lastly we covered Multi-row functions such as *count*, *avg* and *sum*. It is important to remember that multi row functions skip rows where the expression is NULL. Remember that the distinct clause can be added to many of the multi-row functions to remove duplicate values.

At this point, we have the tools we need to manipulate the data returned by our SQL queries. In the next chapter, we will cover sorting, grouping, joining tables and sub queries.

Sorting, Grouping and Table Joins

Mommy! My sub-query's not sorting right!

Sorting, Grouping, Table Joins and Subqueries

In this chapter, we are going to cover sorting the returned rows and using grouping functions to allow the use of multi-row functions on each group. We will then move to joining tables to retrieve data that has been normalized into multiple tables. Finally, we will introduce queries within queries or subqueries. First, we start with sorting our returned rows.

Sorting

Sometimes you want the rows returned from your query to be in a specific order. For example, I might want scores from high to low or names in alphabetical order. By default, the database will sort data ascending, smallest to largest. Words are sorted alphabetically. NULLs cannot be sorted, so they are listed as found at the bottom of the results.

To sort the results set, we use the ORDER BY clause.

```
select
  author_last_name
from
  author
order by author_last_name;
```

If you require that the rows be sorted, you must use the ORDER BY clause, because the Oracle database, by default, will not sort the results set, nor does it store rows in a table in a specific order.

Internally, the Oracle database uses a HEAP organized table as its default table. A HEAP table stores new data in the first available slot. Once you start adding and deleting rows in your table, the row order becomes random. Different queries (and for that matter, the same query run a different times) will use different execution plans to retrieve your requested data. Thus, the results can be ordered differently if you do not use the ORDER BY clause.

Let's look at the AUTHOR table.

```
SQL> select author_key from author;

AUTHOR_KEY
-----------
A101
A102
A103
A104
A105
A106
A107
A108
A109
A110
10 rows selected.
```

The *author_keys* appear to have been sorted. Actually, they were NOT returned sorted. The database simply returned them as it found them when it accessed the author table. Because we loaded the rows in *author_key* order and have not modified the data in the table (no inserts, deletes, etc), the return appears sorted. Once we start making changes to the data, it will no longer appear sorted.

The only way to insure that the rows are ordered the way you want them is have the query specify the sorting using the ORDER BY clause. Also, sorting is always performed last. It makes no sense to sort an intermediate row set that we will never see.

Sorting is expensive to the database, and so you want to sort the smallest number of rows, which is the final row set. Sometimes, you will want to sort a subset, such as the results of a sub query, but normally you will sort once at the end of the query.

Subqueries are covered later in this chapter. The good news is that the database takes care of the mechanics of sorting for you. So, let's look at the ORDER BY clause.

```
Select
  author_last_name
from
  author;

AUTHOR_LAST_NAME
---------------------------------------
jones
hester
weaton
jeckle
withers
petty
clark
mee
shagger
smith
10 rows selected.
```

```
Select
  author_last_name
from
  author
order by author_last_name;

AUTHOR_LAST_NAME
----------------------------------------
clark
hester
jeckle
jones
mee
petty
shagger
smith
weaton
withers

10 rows selected.
```

In the first query, we retrieved the *author_last_name* from the author table. The rows were returned as the database found them. In the second example, we executed the same query except that we used the ORDER BY clause to order them alphabetically by last name. Notice that the default is ascending. In the next example, we again selected the author's last name but we ordered them by *author_key* descending.

```
Select
  author_last_name
from
  author
order by author_key desc;

AUTHOR_LAST_NAME
----------------------------------------
smith
shagger
mee
clark
petty
withers
jeckle
weaton
hester
jones

10 rows selected.
```

Notice in the example above that I did not select the *author_key* even though I used it in my ORDER BY clause.

Multi-column Sorting

You can also sort by multiple columns. In this case, the rows are sorted by the first column listed, then sorted within the first column by the second column, then within the second column by the third column and so forth.

```
SQL> select
  2     order_number o,
  3     store_key s,
  4     book_key b
  5  from
  6     sales
  7  order by b,s;

O                    S    B
-------------------- ---- ------
O101                 S101 B101
O129                 S103 B101
O199                 S104 B101
O196                 S105 B101
O168                 S110 B101
O102                 S102 B102
O103                 S103 B102
O130                 S103 B102
O104                 S104 B102
O105                 S105 B102
O197                 S106 B102
O146                 S107 B102
O183                 S107 B102
O109                 S109 B102
O110                 S110 B102
O167                 S110 B102
O198                 S102 B103
O131                 S103 B103
O106                 S106 B103
O107                 S107 B103
O184                 S107 B103
O148                 S107 B103
O108                 S108 B103
```

Notice that in our ORDER BY clause (on line eight) we used an alias for column name. Using alias names saves typing and also makes complex SQL easier to read. I can sort by the column name, the column alias, or the column position.

```
SQL> Select
  2      order_number,
  3      store_key,
  4      book_key
  5  from
  6      sales
  7  order by 3, 2;

ORDER_NUMBER               STOR BOOK_K
--------------------       ---- ------
O101                       S101 B101
O129                       S103 B101
O199                       S104 B101
O196                       S105 B101
O168                       S110 B101
O102                       S102 B102
O103                       S103 B102
O130                       S103 B102
O104                       S104 B102
O105                       S105 B102
O197                       S106 B102
O146                       S107 B102
O183                       S107 B102
O109                       S109 B102
O110                       S110 B102
O167                       S110 B102
O198                       S102 B103
O131                       S103 B103
```

However, you cannot use column position if you union or minus multiple queries together.

Finally, sorting is an expensive operation for the database. The Oracle database will try to sort the results in memory, but if the results set is large, the database must sort to disk and pay the very high I/O cost. You should only sort your results if you require the rows in a certain order.

Sorting using the ORDER BY clause is performed on the entire set of returned rows. But what if we want the rows divided into groups and then have multi-row functions applied to each group? What if we want to get a list of the average sales quantity per order by store? I would have to separately query for the average of each store, or I can query all the rows, group them by store and then apply my AVG function. For this, I use a clause called GROUP BY.

Grouping Related Rows

Grouping is a special type of sorting. With sorting, all the rows are sorted by the columns specified. Grouping sorts the rows into groups so that multi row functions can be specified at the group level.

```
SQL> select
  avg(quantity)
from
  sales;

AVG(QUANTITY)
-------------
      1105B5

select
  store_key,
  avg(quantity)
from
  sales
group by store_key;
```

The first example uses the average function to provide us the average sales for all orders. The second example provides the average quantity for each store. The database sorts the rows into groups, with one group per store key. It then feeds the groups, one at a time to the average function that computes the average for that group. The GROUP BY clause can be used with multiple columns and with multiple functions.

```
SQL> select
  2    store_key,
  3    book_key,
  4    sum(quantity) total,
  5    avg(quantity) Average,
  6    count(quantity) Num
  7  from
  8    sales
  9  group by store_key, book_key;
```

```
STOR  BOOK_K      TOTAL     AVERAGE          NUM
----  ------  ----------  ----------   ----------
S101  B101          1000        1000            1
S101  B114           900         900            1
S101  B115           180         180            1
S101  B116           100         100            1
S102  B102            10          10            1
S102  B103          8900        8900            1
S102  B110          1400         700            2
S102  B111          1400         700            2
S102  B112           600         300            2
S102  B113           500         500            1
S102  B114           150         150            1
S102  B115          8800        8800            1
S102  B116           100         100            1
S103  B101           100         100            1
S103  B102           400         200            2
```

This example groups the retrieved records by *store_key* and *book_key*. It then computes the average and total quantities for each group. Lastly, it counts the number of rows in that group.

When you use the GROUP BY clause, you must include all columns in the SELECT clause. Otherwise, you will get the error below (I removed the *book_key*).

```
SQL> select
  2     store_key,
  3     book_key,
  4     sum(quantity) total,
  5     avg(quantity) Average,
  6     count(quantity) Num
  7  from
  8     sales
  9  group by store_key;
   book_key,
   *
ERROR at line 3:
ORA-00979: not a GROUP BY expression
```

Here, the database is saying that the *book_key* is not part of the GROUP BY clause. You can, however, include columns in the GROUP BY clause that are not in the SELECT clause.

```
SQL> select
  2     sum(quantity) total,
  3     avg(quantity) Average,
  4     count(quantity) Num
```

```
  5  from
  6    sales
  7  group by store_key, book_key;

      TOTAL    AVERAGE         NUM
---------- ---------- ----------
      1000       1000           1
       900        900           1
       180        180           1
       100        100           1
        10         10           1
      8900       8900           1
      1400        700           2
      1400        700           2
       600        300           2
       ...
```

All columns listed in the SELECT clause that are not in a function must be included in the GROUP BY clause. This is an ANSI SQL requirement.

We need a way to limit the returned rows after the grouping has been applied, such as rows with sum(quantity) less that 500. We can't use the WHERE clause because it is used to limit the row set returned before the grouping takes place, so when Oracle applies this limit, the sum(quantity) has not yet been calculated.

```
SQL> select
  2    sum(quantity) Qty
  3  from
  4    sales
  5  where sum(quantity) < 400
  6  group by store_key, book_key;
where sum(quantity) < 400
      *
ERROR at line 5:
ORA-00934: group function is not allowed here
```

To limit the returned rows after the grouping, we use the HAVING clause. The HAVING clause is applied after the grouping has taken place.

```
SQL> select
  2    sum(quantity) Qty
  3  from
  4    sales
```

```
  5  group by store_key, book_key
  6  having sum(quantity) < 400;

       QTY
  ----------
       180
       100
        10
       150
       100
       100
       100

37 rows selected.
```

Your SQL statement can have both a WHERE clause and a
HAVING clause. The WHERE clause filters rows as they are
selected from the table, and before grouping, the HAVING
clause filters rows after the grouping.

The "GROUP BY" Clause can be confusing.

Finally, if we want to order the rows that are returned after
grouping, we add the ORDER BY clause at the end.

```
SQL> select
  2    sum(quantity) Qty
  3  from
  4    sales
  5  group by store_key, book_key
  6  having sum(quantity) < 400
  7  order by Qty;
```

```
       QTY
----------
        10
       100
       100
       100
  ...
       100
       150
       180
       180
       200
       200
       300
       300
       300
```

37 rows selected.

Because of our grouping, we can only order the results set on an identifier that exists after the grouping, in our case *store_key*, *book_key* or Qty. If we tried to use *order_number*, we would get an error because the *order_number* has no definition once we have grouped the rows.

Now that we have our results returned in the order we want, it is time start including data from multiple tables. For this, we need to join the tables together.

Table Joins

Joining tables together is one of the most important aspects of SQL, and it is the tool that allows the relationships which give relational databases their name. Let's take a simple example and see how joins work.

Well our boss is at it again. He wants a list of stores in South Carolina that sell our books and the title of the books each store has sold. The basic information is in the SALES table.

```
SQL> desc sales
 Name                            Null?    Type
 ------------------------------- -------- --------------------
 STORE_KEY                                VARCHAR2(4)
 BOOK_KEY                                 VARCHAR2(6)
 ORDER_NUMBER                             VARCHAR2(20)
 ORDER_DATE                               DATE
 QUANTITY                                 NUMBER(5)
```

What we are looking for is a list of *store_keys* (stores) and the *book_keys* (books) that they have sold.

```
SQL> select distinct
  2     store_key,
  3     book_key
  4  from
  5     sales
  6  order by store_key,book_key;

STOR BOOK_K
---- ------
S101 B101
S101 B114
S101 B115
S101 B116
S102 B102
S102 B103
S102 B110
S102 B111
S102 B112
...
S109 B116
S110 B101
S110 B102
S110 B103
S110 B104
S110 B105
S110 B106

80 rows selected.
```

We can only get so far with the data in the SALES table. We will need to include the STORE table to get the store name and to determine which stores are located in South Carolina.

```
SQL> desc store
 Name                            Null?    Type
 ----------------------- -------- ------------------------
 STORE_KEY                                VARCHAR2(4)
 STORE_NAME                               VARCHAR2(40)
 STORE_ADDRESS                            VARCHAR2(40)
 STORE_CITY                               VARCHAR2(20)
 STORE_STATE                              VARCHAR2(2)
 STORE_ZIP                                VARCHAR2(5)
```

From the description of the STORE table above, we can see that we can get the store name and state using the store key. In relational terms, the SALES table is related to the store table using the *store_key* (Figure 3.1).

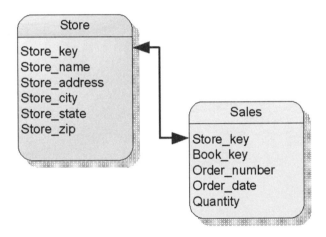

Figure 3.1: Joining the Store and Sales Tables

The *store_key* is common to both tables, and we will use it to relate the two tables. Starting with the query we just created, we will replace the *store_key* with the store name.

```
SQL> select distinct
  2    store_name,
  3    book_key
  4  from
  5    sales, store
  6  where
  7    store.store_key = sales.store_key
  8  order by store_name,book_key;
```

```
STORE_NAME                                 BOOK_K
---------------------------------------    ------
barnes and Noble                           B101
barnes and Noble                           B114
barnes and Noble                           B115
barnes and Noble                           B116
blue ride booksellers                      B103
blue ride booksellers                      B107
blue ride booksellers                      B108
...
wee bee books                              B111
wee bee books                              B114
wee bee books                              B115
wee bee books                              B116

80 rows selected.
```

This is the most Oracle standard syntax for a join, where you manually tell the SQL the join keys.

Natural Join

You can also use the ANSI SQL syntax, which in many cases is easier to understand. The ANSI natural join tells the database to join the two tables on the common columns.

```
select distinct
  store_name,
  book_key
from
  sales natural join store
order by store_name,book_key;
```

While the natural join appears to be easy, I personally do not like it because it is relying on the database to determine which columns are the join columns. I prefer to identify them in the query. It is easier to troubleshoot and easier for someone else to look at your query and understand what it is doing. The second ANSI join format is very much like the original example except that all the join information is located in the FROM clause leaving the WHERE clause exclusively for filtering.

```
select distinct
  store_name,
  book_key
```

```
from
  sales join store on (store.store_key = sales.store_key)
order by store_name,book_key;
```

This format is cleaner to read and understand, especially as the queries get more complicated.

The boss only wants those stores from South Carolina, so we need to add the filter.

```
SQL> select distinct
  2     store_name,
  3     book_key
  4  from
        sales join store on (store.store_key = sales.store_key)
  5  where
        store_state = 'SC'
  6  order by store_name,book_key;

STORE_NAME                                  BOOK_K
------------------------------------------  ------
eaton books                                 B102
eaton books                                 B104
eaton books                                 B106
eaton books                                 B107
eaton books                                 B108
eaton books                                 B109
eaton books                                 B113
eaton books                                 B116
hot wet and mushy books                     B102
hot wet and mushy books                     B103
hot wet and mushy books                     B104
hot wet and mushy books                     B105
hot wet and mushy books                     B106
hot wet and mushy books                     B107
hot wet and mushy books                     B108
hot wet and mushy books                     B109
hot wet and mushy books                     B110
hot wet and mushy books                     B111

18 rows selected.
```

Almost there! The boss also wants the book titles, not the *book_key*. For that, we will have to join to BOOK table into our query. The BOOK table joins the SALES table on the *book_key*.

```
SQL> desc book
 Name                              Null?    Type
 --------------------------------- -------- ----------------------------
 BOOK_KEY                                   VARCHAR2(6)
 PUB_KEY                                    VARCHAR2(4)
 BOOK_TITLE                                 VARCHAR2(80)
 BOOK_TYPE                                  VARCHAR2(30)
 BOOK_RETAIL_PRICE                          VARCHAR2(30)
 BOOK_ADVANCES                              VARCHAR2(30)
 BOOK_ROYALTIES                             NUMBER(10)
 BOOK_YTD_SALES                             NUMBER(10)
 BOOK_COMMENTS                              VARCHAR2(200)
 BOOK_DATE_PUBLISHED                        DATE
```

So, we are going to join the SALES, STORE and BOOK tables together using the *store_key* and the *book_key* as shown in Figure 3.2. The change to our query is minor, just add the join to the FROM clause and change the *book_key* to *book_*title in the SELECT and ORDER BY clauses.

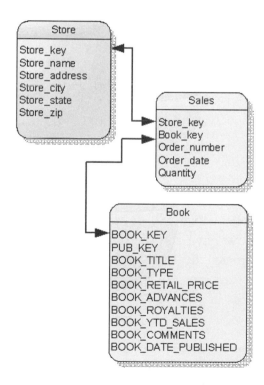

Figure 3.2: *Joining the STORE, SALES and BOOK Tables*

```
SQL> select distinct
  2     store_name,
  3     book_title
  4  from
  5     sales join store on (store.store_key = sales.store_key),
  6           join book  on (sales.book_key = book.book_key)
  7  where
        store_state = 'SC'
  8  order by store_name,book_title;

STORE_NAME
----------------------------------------
BOOK_TITLE
------------------------------------------------------------------
eaton books
DOS for dummies

eaton books
The zen of auto repair

eaton books
UNIX for experts

eaton books
bears are people too

eaton books
managing stress

eaton books
non violins in the workplace

eaton books
operations research theory
...
hot wet and mushy books
zero loss finance

32 rows selected.
```

Well, we got the information but we will never get a raise giving the boss that. Since we now have the query, let's clean up the formatting, and since we know the boss will be asking for the same report on another stats in the future, we will add a SQL*Plus variable to filter the state.

🖫 store_state.sql

```
-- ****************************************************
-- Copyright © 2005 by Rampant TechPress
-- This script is free for non-commercial purposes
```

```
-- with no warranties.  Use at your own risk.
--
-- To license this script for a commercial purpose,
-- contact info@rampant.cc
-- *************************************************

-- Books, By Store, Filter by State
-- store_state.sql

set pages 999 line 74 feedback off verify off

accept statecode prompt "Enter a State: "

column c1 heading "Store Name" format a28
column c2 heading "Book Title" format a34

select distinct
  initcap (store_name) c1,
  initcap (book_title) c2
from
  sales join store on (store.store_key = sales.store_key)
        join book  on (sales.book_key = book.book_key)
where
  store_state = '&statecode'
order by c1,c2;

set feedback on verify on
clear columns
```

In this example, I used the SQL*Plus ACCEPT command to prompt the user for a state and store the results in a variable called statecode. The query then uses the statecode variable in the WHERE clause. When I run the script and enter SC for the state, I get the results below.

```
SQL> @store_state
Enter a State: SC

Store Name                   Book Title
---------------------------  ----------------------------------
Eaton Books                  Bears Are People Too
Eaton Books                  Dos For Dummies
Eaton Books                  Managing Stress
Eaton Books                  Non Violins In The Workplace
Eaton Books                  Operations Research Theory
Eaton Books                  Oracle9i Sql Tuning
Eaton Books                  Pay No Taxes And Go To Jail
Eaton Books                  Piano Greats
Eaton Books                  Reduce Spending The Republican Way
Eaton Books                  The Fall Of Microsoft
Eaton Books                  The Willow Weeps No More
Eaton Books                  The Zen Of Auto Repair
```

```
Eaton Books                  Unix For Experts
Eaton Books                  Windows Success
Eaton Books                  Writers Market
Eaton Books                  Zero Loss Finance
Hot Wet And Mushy Books      Bears Are People Too
Hot Wet And Mushy Books      Dos For Dummies
Hot Wet And Mushy Books      Managing Stress
Hot Wet And Mushy Books      Non Violins In The Workplace
Hot Wet And Mushy Books      Operations Research Theory
Hot Wet And Mushy Books      Oracle9i Sql Tuning
Hot Wet And Mushy Books      Pay No Taxes And Go To Jail
Hot Wet And Mushy Books      Piano Greats
Hot Wet And Mushy Books      Reduce Spending The Republican Way
Hot Wet And Mushy Books      The Fall Of Microsoft
Hot Wet And Mushy Books      The Willow Weeps No More
Hot Wet And Mushy Books      The Zen Of Auto Repair
Hot Wet And Mushy Books      Unix For Experts
Hot Wet And Mushy Books      Windows Success
Hot Wet And Mushy Books      Writers Market
Hot Wet And Mushy Books      Zero Loss Finance
```

This report is acceptable, but remember, we are going for the raise.

The SQL*Plus Break Command

I can add some flash to this report by using the SQL*Plus BREAK command. The BREAK command tells SQL*Plus to print a column once, then wait for the column to change. Each time the column changes, SQL*Plus will print the new value once after skipping the defined number of lines. Since this is another SQL*Plus command, it goes before the query in our script. I am going to implement the BREAK command on the Store Name and skip two lines between stores.

🖫 **state_report.sql**

```
-- Books, By Store, Filter by State, with Break
-- state_report.sql

set pages 999 line 74 feedback off verify off

accept statecode prompt "Enter a State: "

column c1 heading "Store Name" format a28
column c2 heading "Book Title" format a34

break on c1 skip 2

select distinct
  initcap (store_name) c1,
  initcap (book_title) c2
from
  sales join store on (store.store_key = sales.store_key)
       join book  on (sales.book_key = book.book_key)
where
  store_state = '&statecode'
order by c1,c2;

set feedback on verify on
clear columns
```

Executing the script produces the report below.

```
SQL> @store_state
Enter a State:SC

Store Name                   Book Title
---------------------------- ----------------------------------
Eaton Books                  Bears Are People Too
                             Dos For Dummies
                             Managing Stress
                             Non Violins In The Workplace
                             Operations Research Theory
                             Oracle9i Sql Tuning
                             Pay No Taxes And Go To Jail
                             Piano Greats
                             Reduce Spending The Republican Way
                             The Fall Of Microsoft
                             The Willow Weeps No More
                             The Zen Of Auto Repair
                             Unix For Experts
                             Windows Success
                             Writers Market
                             Zero Loss Finance

Hot Wet And Mushy Books      Bears Are People Too
                             Dos For Dummies
                             Managing Stress
                             Non Violins In The Workplace
                             Operations Research Theory
                             Oracle9i Sql Tuning
```

```
Pay No Taxes And Go To Jail
Piano Greats
Reduce Spending The Republican Way
The Fall Of Microsoft
The Willow Weeps No More
The Zen Of Auto Repair
Unix For Experts
Windows Success
Writers Market
Zero Loss Finance
```

So, joins are how we get data from multiple tables. I introduced a lot of items in the examples above, so let's quickly review the joins.

The standard Oracle join format list the tables in the FROM clause and the join criteria in the WHERE clause.

```
select distinct
  store_name,
  book_key
from
  sales, store
where
  store.store_key = sales.store_key
order by store_name,book_key;
```

Using the ANSI SQL format, the tables and the join criteria are listed in the FROM clause.

```
select distinct
  store_name,
  book_key
from
  sales join store on (store.store_key = sales.store_key)
order by store_name,book_key;
```

The ON key word tells the database to limit the returned rows to those where the columns defined match, or don't match in the case of an anti-join. If the join columns have the same name, I can replace the ON clause with the USING clause like below.

```
select distinct
  store_name,
  book_key
from
  sales join store using (store_key)
order by store_name,book_key;
```

Here, both tables have a column called *store_key*, and we are using them to join the tables. We will discuss the USING clause more when we talk about natural joins later in the chapter.

There are a number of different types of joins and each is used for a specific purpose. Let's look at the different types of table joins.

Cartesian Product

The Cartesian product, also referred to as a cross-join, returns all the rows in all the tables listed in the query. Each row in the first table is paired with all the rows in the second table. This happens then there is no relationship defined between the two tables. Both the AUTHOR and STORE tables have ten rows. If we use a Cartesian join in these two tables, we will get back 100 rows.

```
SQL> select
  2     author_key,
  3     store_key
  4   from
  5     author, store;

AUTHOR_KEY  STOR
----------- ----
A101        S101
A101        S102
A101        S103
A101        S104
A101        S105
A101        S106
A101        S107
A101        S108
A101        S109
A101        S110
A102        S101
A102        S102
...
A110        S105
```

```
A110        S106
A110        S107
A110        S108
A110        S109
A110        S110

100 rows selected.
```

Most of the time, we do not want a Cartesian join, and we end up with one because we failed to provide a filter on the join. If we actually want a Cartesian join, then we should use the ANSI cross join to tell others reading the script that we actually wanted a Cartesian join.

```
select
  author_key,
  store_key
from
  author cross join store;
```

One reason to use a Cartesian join is to generate a large amount of rows to use for testing. I can take a large table and cross join it to another large table and produce a very large results set. If I cross join *dba_objects* and *dba_views*, I can produce the results set below.

```
SQL> select count(*)
  2  from
  3    dba_objects cross join dba_views;

  COUNT(*)
----------
 164623840
```

That's a lot of rows!

Remember, if you forget to specify your join criteria, you may get a Cartesian result!

Most of the time, we will want to join our tables on some meaningful key. SQL provides a number of join methods, like the natural join, relate multiple tables. While the natural join can be confusing and possibly error prone, the equal join clearly defines how we want to join our table and on what columns.

Equality Joins

In an equality join, the tables are related using the equals (=) sign. This is the most common join and was used in the example at the beginning of this section. Basically, an equal join will compare the related values and return only those joined rows where they are the same.

```
SQL> select
  2      author_last_name,
  3      book_title
  4    from
  5      author a join book_author ba on (a.author_key =
ba.author_key)
  6              join book b          on (ba.book_key = b.book_key);

AUTHOR_LAST_NAME               BOOK_TITLE
------------------------------ ---------------------------------------
hester                         windows success
jones                          windows success
jeckle                         piano greats
weaton                         piano greats
withers                        DOS for dummies
shagger                        The zen of auto repair
smith                          zero loss finance
jeckle                         operations research theory
shagger                        non violins in the workplace
weaton                         UNIX for experts
hester                         pay no taxes and go to jail
jeckle                         the fall of microsoft
shagger                        writers market
smith                          managing stress
shagger                        bears are people too
weaton                         reduce spending the republican way
petty                          the willow weeps no more
hester                         oracle9i sql tuning
shagger                        was george washington feeble?
jones                          was george washington feeble?
jones                          cooking light
jones                          never eat meat
withers                        never eat meat
weaton                         never eat meat
shagger                        how to housebreak your horse

25 rows selected.
```

Remember that a book can have more than one author.

One ANSI join that is a type of equality join is the natural join. A natural join is where tables are joined by matching column names and column values. As stated earlier, I do not like this join because it allows the database to determine the matching columns. To me, it is ambiguous to the code reader. Here is the query above rewritten using a natural join.

```
select
  author_last_name,
  book_title
from
  author natural join book_author natural join book;
```

A problem with the natural join is that I can't use aliases because they change the column names. The below query will execute correctly without problem.

```
select
    author_last_name,
    book_title,
    book_key
from
    author natural join book_author
            natural join book;
```

Using the old Oracle join format, the query above will throw an error stating that *book_key* is ambiguous because it is in both the BOOK and *book_author* table. Using the ANSI format, the database knows that it equal joined the tables using *book_key*, so in the rows returned, *book_key* is the same in both tables. If I try to alias *book_key*, I get an error.

```
SQL> select
  2    a.author_last_name,
  3    b.book_title,
  4    ba.book_key
  5  from
  6    author a natural join book_author ba
  7            natural join book b;
```

```
  ba.book_key
  *
ERROR at line 4:
ORA-00904: "BA"."BOOK_KEY": invalid identifier
```

My alias changed the column name for the *book_key* column and confused the database.

What happens when my tables contain columns that match in name but are unsuitable for the join? An example would be a comment column. This column contains text comments and I do not want it in the join. The natural join, however, will use it in the join, unless I exclude it using the USING clause.

```
select
  author_last_name,
  book_title
from
  author join book_author using (author_key)
         join book        using (book_key);
```

Notice that the natural key word is no longer used, and in fact, I am no longer doing a natural join but a standard inner join. The USING clause is added to define the column or columns used to join the tables. Columns not listed are excluded from the join. The USING clause requires that the column names in both tables match. If not, you must use the ON clause and define the equality.

Non-Equality Joins

A non-equality join is not based on the equals (=) sign. Sometimes called an anti-join, non-equality joins include those joins based on <>, <, > and NOT.

```
select
  store_name,
  order_number
from
  store join sales on (store.store_key <> sales.store_key);
```

This example gives us the Cartesian join minus the equal join, thus the name anti-join. Remember, the non-equal join is talking about joining the tables, not filtering the row, that is still the job of the WHERE clause.

Outer Joins

With the equal join, you get all the rows where the comparison is equal. Sometimes, you want all the rows in one table and the matching rows in the other table.

Outer joins can magically make missing rows appear

For example, if I list my authors and the books they have written, I get the results below.

```
SQL> select
  2    author_last_name,
  3    book_key
  4  from
  5    author join book_author using (author_key)
  6  order by author_last_name;
```

```
AUTHOR_LAST_NAME                          BOOK_K
---------------------------------------   ------
hester                                    B101
hester                                    B109
hester                                    B116
jeckle                                    B102
jeckle                                    B110
jeckle                                    B106
jones                                     B101
jones                                     B119
jones                                     B117
jones                                     B118
petty                                     B115
shagger                                   B104
shagger                                   B111
shagger                                   B113
shagger                                   B120
shagger                                   B117
shagger                                   B107
smith                                     B105
smith                                     B112
weaton                                    B102
weaton                                    B108
weaton                                    B114
weaton                                    B119
withers                                   B103
withers                                   B119

25 rows selected.
```

The problem with this listing is that there are ten authors in the author table and only eight listed. The remaining two authors have not yet written a book.

Always check to make sure that join rows are not missing.

What if I wanted the listing to include these two authors? Because they do not match the equal join, I will need to use an outer join. An outer join will include all rows from the outer table and those matching rows from the other table. Rows that are included from the outer table that have no match in the other table will have NULLs in those columns.

```
SQL> select
  2     author_last_name,
  3     book_key
  4  from
  5     author left outer join book_author using (author_key)
  6  order by author_last_name;

AUTHOR_LAST_NAME                         BOOK_K
---------------------------------------- ------
clark
hester                                   B101
hester                                   B109
hester                                   B116
jeckle                                   B102
jeckle                                   B110
jeckle                                   B106
jones                                    B101
jones                                    B119
jones                                    B117
jones                                    B118
mee
petty                                    B115
shagger                                  B104
shagger                                  B111
shagger                                  B113
shagger                                  B120
shagger                                  B117
shagger                                  B107
smith                                    B105
smith                                    B112
weaton                                   B102
weaton                                   B108
weaton                                   B114
weaton                                   B119
withers                                  B103
withers                                  B119

27 rows selected.
```

In the example above, the AUTHOR table is on the left, and we are using a left outer join, so we get all the rows in the AUTHOR table and the matching rows in the *book_author* table. Notice that both authors clark and mee now are listed, and the *book_key* column is NULL. In the standard Oracle format, outer joins can be confusing. Below is the same query in the standard Oracle format.

```
select
  author_last_name,
  book_key
from
  author,
  book_author
where
  author.author_key = book_author.author_key(+)
order by author_last_name;
```

Notice the (+) in the WHERE clause. This indicates a left outer join. If we were using a right outer join, the WHERE clause would be:

```
author.author_key(+) = book_author.author_key
```

Here, all the rows from the *book_author* table would be included and the missing rows from the AUTHOR table would be NULL. The example below demonstrates the ANSI right outer join.

```
SQL> select
  2    author_last_name,
  3    book_key
  4  from
  5    author right outer join book_author using (author_key)
  6  order by author_last_name;
```

```
AUTHOR_LAST_NAME                            BOOK_K
---------------------------------------     ------
hester                                      B116
hester                                      B109
hester                                      B101
jeckle                                      B110
jeckle                                      B102
jeckle                                      B106
jones                                       B119
jones                                       B118
jones                                       B117
jones                                       B101
petty                                       B115
shagger                                     B120
shagger                                     B111
shagger                                     B117
shagger                                     B113
shagger                                     B107
shagger                                     B104
smith                                       B112
smith                                       B105
weaton                                      B119
weaton                                      B114
weaton                                      B108
weaton                                      B102
withers                                     B119
withers                                     B103
                                            B122
                                            B121
27 rows selected.
```

Here we see two planned books that do not yet have authors; *book_key*s 121 and 122.

Sometimes, you want to include all rows in both tables. The ANSI SQL format can do this using the full outer join.

```
SQL> select
  2    author_last_name,
  3    book_key
  4  from
  5    author full outer join book_author using (author_key)
  6  order by author_last_name;
```

```
AUTHOR_LAST_NAME                              BOOK_K
---------------------------------------       ------
clark
hester                                        B101
hester                                        B109
hester                                        B116
jeckle                                        B102
jeckle                                        B110
jeckle                                        B106
jones                                         B101
jones                                         B119
jones                                         B117
jones                                         B118
mee
petty                                         B115
shagger                                       B104
shagger                                       B111
shagger                                       B113
shagger                                       B120
shagger                                       B117
shagger                                       B107
smith                                         B105
smith                                         B112
weaton                                        B102
weaton                                        B108
weaton                                        B114
weaton                                        B119
withers                                       B103
withers                                       B119
                                              B122
                                              B121
29 rows selected.
```

Notice that the results included the unpublished authors (clark and mee) and the books not yet assigned to authors (B121 and B122). There is no standard Oracle format for a full outer join. You must union a left and right outer join to get the same results.

```
SQL> select
  2     author_last_name,
  3     book_key
  4  from
  5     author,
  6     book_author
  7  where
  8     author.author_key = book_author.author_key(+)
  9  union
 10   select
 11     author_last_name,
 12     book_key
 13  from
 14     author,
 15     book_author
```

```
 16  where
 17    author.author_key(+) = book_author.author_key
 18  order by author_last_name;

AUTHOR_LAST_NAME                          BOOK_K
----------------------------------------- ------
clark
hester                                    B101
hester                                    B109
hester                                    B116
jeckle                                    B102
jeckle                                    B106
jeckle                                    B110
jones                                     B101
jones                                     B117
jones                                     B118
jones                                     B119
mee
petty                                     B115
shagger                                   B104
shagger                                   B107
shagger                                   B111
shagger                                   B113
shagger                                   B117
shagger                                   B120
smith                                     B105
smith                                     B112
weaton                                    B102
weaton                                    B108
weaton                                    B114
weaton                                    B119
withers                                   B103
withers                                   B119
                                          B121
                                          B122
29 rows selected.
```

Notice that the union removed duplicate rows, and I only ordered the results set once at the end of the query.

Self Join

A self join is used to join a table to itself, and it is commonly used when you have a table with dates and you want to compare one date to another within the same table.

Self-joins can get ugly

Visually, it sometimes helps to look at the table as two identical tables (A and B). I am joining A to B, it just happens to be the same table. Because the table is used twice in the query, you must alias the table, and of course, you cannot use a natural join. In the example below, I want a list of employees and their managers. In the EMP table, each employee is identified by an *emp_key*. The employee's manager is in the manager column and it contains the manager's *emp_key*.

```
SQL> select
  2    b.emp_last_name EMPLOYEE,
  3    a.emp_last_name MANAGER
  4  from
  5    emp a right outer join emp b on (a.emp_key = b.manager);

EMPLOYEE                      MANAGER
----------------------------- -----------------------------
brannigan                     king
coleman                       king
baker                         king
johnson                       king
levender                      king
tokheim                       king
linus                         king
korn                          king
jackson                       king
king

10 rows selected
```

As you can see, King is the manager for each of the employees, and King does not have a manager assigned. I used an outer join so that King would also be listed as an employee, even though he has no manager. Otherwise, King would not have been listed. I join the *emp* table to itself, joining where the *emp_key* matched the manager.

Multi-table Joins

Multi-table joins can become confusing and this is where the ANSI format really shines. By keeping all the join information out of the WHERE clause, it is much easier to read as the query becomes more complicated. Using the ANSI format, you can also outer join multiple tables with multiple outer joins. That was not allowed in the standard Oracle format.

```
SQL> select
  2     author_last_name c1,
  3     book_title       c2
  4  from
  5     author full outer join book_author using (author_key)
  6             full outer join book using (book_key)
  7  order by author_last_name;

Author                       Title
------------------------     -----------------------------------
clark
hester                       windows success
hester                       pay no taxes and go to jail
hester                       oracle9i sql tuning
jeckle                       piano greats
jeckle                       the fall of microsoft
jeckle                       operations research theory
jones                        windows success
jones                        never eat meat
jones                        was george washington feeble?
jones                        cooking light
mee
petty                        the willow weeps no more
shagger                      The zen of auto repair
shagger                      writers market
shagger                      bears are people too
shagger                      how to housebreak your horse
shagger                      was george washington feeble?
shagger                      non violins in the workplace
smith                        zero loss finance
smith                        managing stress
```

138

```
weaton                     piano greats
weaton                     never eat meat
weaton                     UNIX for experts
weaton                     reduce spending the republican way
withers                    DOS for dummies
withers                    never eat meat
                           fired - now what
                           the far side of the goon

29 rows selected.
```

In the example above, I joined three tables using full outer joins. This allowed me to include both the books without authors and the authors without books in my report. Note: I had to remove the *book_keys* that did not have *author_keys* from the *book author* table for this example.

When joining multiple tables, the joins are performed from left to right. Each successive table on the right can use the columns resulting from the joins to its left. You can also mix the use of the ON and USING clause in your joins.

We now have the ability to link our tables and retrieve information from multiple tables. But what if you do not want to use the entire table? A subquery gives use the ability to create a subset of data, that is then used in our main query.

Subqueries

Subqueries are queries within queries. They can exist in almost any part of the main query to include the SELECT, FROM, WHERE and HAVING clauses. In the SELECT clause, a subquery can return a value that becomes a column in your results.

```
SQL> select
  2    author_last_name,
  3    book_title,
  4    (select
  5      max(order_date)
  6    from
  7      sales) "Last Order"
```

```
8   from
9     author a join book_author ba using (author_key)
10              join book b        using (book_key);

AUTHOR_LAST_NAME
-----------------------------------------
BOOK_TITLE
--------------------------------------------------------------------
Last Orde
---------
hester
windows success
21-MAY-04

jones
windows success
21-MAY-04

jeckle
piano greats
21-MAY-04

weaton
piano greats
21-MAY-04
...
```

The subquery returns the max order date from the sales table. Notice that the sub query returns a single value.

A subquery in the FROM clause will create a table in memory that can be used by the outer query to select from.

```
SQL> select
  2     name,
  3     sum(quantity)
  4  from
  5     sales join (select
  6                   store_name name,
  7                   store_key  key
  8                 from
  9                 store) str on (sales.store_key = str.key)
 10  group by name;
```

```
NAME                                       SUM(QUANTITY)
---------------------------------------- --------------
barnes and Noble                                  2180
blue ride booksellers                             5400
books for dummies                                13000
borders                                          21860
eaton books                                      12120
hot wet and mushy books                          24700
ignoramus and dufus                               3610
quagmire books                                    7900
specialty bookstore                               6080
wee bee books                                    13700

10 rows selected.
```

Here, my subquery becomes the table STR for the outer query. Subqueries in the FROM clause can be sorted. Subqueries in other clauses cannot contain an ORDER BY clause.

The most common place for a subquery is in the WHERE clause.

```
SQL> select
  2     store_key,
  3     book_key
  4  from
  5     sales
  6  where
  7     book_key in (select
  8                     book_key
  9                  from
 10                     book_author
 11                  where
 12                     author_key  in ('A101','A103','A106'));
STOR BOOK_K
---- ------
S104 B101
S105 B101
S110 B101
S103 B101
S101 B101
S106 B102
S107 B102
S110 B102
...
S102 B114
S101 B114
S102 B115
S104 B115
S104 B115
S106 B115
S101 B115
32 rows selected.
```

Here my subquery provided a list of *book_key* to use in filtering the outer query's results. This subquery returned multiple values.

As you can see, subqueries can be a very powerful feature of SQL; however, it can also cause your SQL to be confusing and to perform poorly. A subquery follows the format of a normal SELECT query statement, but it is contained in parentheses and does not end in a semicolon. Subqueries can be nested to any level. The inner most suquery is evaluated first. As we have seen in the examples above, a subquery can return a single row or multiple rows. Each type of subquery must be handled correctly for the query to execute correctly.

Single Row Subquery

A single row subquery returns only one row. It can be used with the equal comparison operators (=,<,>,<>, etc).

```
SQL> select
  2     order_number
  3  from
  4     sales
  5  where quantity = (select
  6                       max(quantity)
  7                     from
  8                       sales);

ORDER_NUMBER
--------------------
0161
```

Here, we get the order number for the order that contains the max quantity value. The outer query can return multiply rows, but the subquery can only return one row.

```
SQL> select
  2     order_number
  3  from
  4     sales
```

```
   5   where quantity > (select
   6                      avg(quantity)
   7                 from
   8                   sales);

ORDER_NUMBER
--------------------
O118
O149
O157
O161
O167
O179
O183
O186
O189
O193
O196
O197
O198
O199

14 rows selected.
```

Here, we want the order numbers where the order quantity is above the average quantity in the sales table. Notice that the subquery returns one and only one row that used in the filter.

Multi Row Subqueries

A multi row subquery returns one or more rows. Since it returns multiple values, the query must use the set comparison operators (IN,ALL,ANY). If you use a multi row subquery with the equals comparison operators, the database will return an error if more than one row is returned. I am looking for all the *book_key* values that have been sold in South Carolina

```
SQL> select
   2    book_key
   3  from
   4    sales
   5  where
   6    store_key = (select
   7                   store_key
   8                 from
   9                   store
  10                 where store_state = 'SC');
```

```
     store_key = (select
                 *
ERROR at line 6:
ORA-01427: single-row subquery returns more than one row
```

In the example above, the subquery returns multiple rows, so the outer query could not evaluate the equals sign. All I need to do is change the equals sign to a set operator.

```
SQL> select
  2     book_key
  3  from
  4     sales
  5  where
  6     store_key in (select
  7                      store_key
  8                   from
  9                      store
 10                   where store_state = 'SC');

BOOK_K
------
B111
B110
B103
B102
...
B116
B106
B102
26 rows selected.
```

The IN operator returns TRUE if the comparison value is contained in the list; in this case, the results of the subquery. The ANY and ALL operators work with the equal operators. The ANY operator returns TRUE if the comparison value matches any of the values in the list. The ALL operator returns TRUE only if the comparison value matches all the values in the list.

```
SQL> select
  2     book_key
  3  from
  4     sales
  5  where
  6     store_key = ANY (select
  7                         store_key
  8                      from
  9                         store
 10                      where store_state = 'SC');
```

```
BOOK_K
------
B111
B110
...
B102

26 rows selected.
```

As you can see, the =ANY comparison is the same as the IN comparison.

```
SQL> select
  2     book_key
  3  from
  4     sales
  5  where
  6     store_key = ALL (select
  7                         store_key
  8                      from
  9                         store
 10                      where store_state = 'SC');

no rows selected
```

Using the ALL operator in the above query will return no rows, since the individual store keys cannot ever match all the store keys in the list. With the IN operator, you can add the NOT operator (NOT IN) to exclude values on the list as opposed to including them.

The difference in single and multi row subqueries is the operator you use in the comparison. Be careful with single row subqueries. Sometimes you will get one row returned because of the data you are developing your query with, but once the query is in use, you may find that it can produce multiple rows, resulting in errors.

Correlated Subqueries

A correlated subquery is a subquery that uses values from the outer query. The Oracle database wants to execute the subquery

---

once and use the results for all the evaluations in the outer query. With a correlated subquery, the database must run the subquery for each evaluation because it is based on the outer query's data.

```
SQL> select
  2     book_key,
  3     store_key,
  4     quantity
  5  from
  6     sales s
  7  where
  8     quantity < (select max(quantity)
  9                    from sales
 10                    where book_key = s.book_key);

BOOK_K STOR   QUANTITY
------ ----  ----------
B101   S101       1000
B102   S102         10
B102   S103        200
...
B116   S105        100
B101   S105       8000
B109   S109        100

81 rows selected.
```

In the example above, the subquery references the *book_key* in the outer query. The value of the *book_key* changes by row of the outer query, so the database must rerun the subquery for each row comparison. This has a significant performance impact on the execution time of the query, and for that reason, correlated subqueries should be avoided if possible.

The outer query knows nothing about the inner query except its results. For that reason, the outer query cannot reference any columns in the subquery. However, the subquery has access to the outer query and can reference outer query columns, thus the correlated subquery.

NULLs in Subqueries

If the subquery returns a NULL as one of its values, it is treated like any other NULL in the database. You cannot compare nor

do math on NULLs. Therefore, if your subquery returns a
NULL, you will need to use the NVL function to handle it.

```
select
  book_key
from
  book_author
where
  author_key in (select
                      NVL(author_key,'A000')
                  from
                      author);
```

In the example above, I used the NVL function to change any
NULL *author_key* into the key A000.

Multi-Column Subqueries

A multi-column subquery is simply a subquery that returns more
than one column.

```
SQL> select
  2    book_key
  3  from
  4    sales
  5    where
  6     (store_key,
  7      order_date) in (select
  8                          store_key,
  9                          max(order_date)
 10                      from
 11                          sales join store using (store_key)
 12                      where
 13                          store_state = 'SC'
 14                      group by store_key);

BOOK_K
------
B111
B109
```

The query lists the books in the latest order from stores in South
Carolina. The subquery returns two columns, a *store_key* and the
date of the latest order. The comparison is a pair-wise
comparison, meaning that the column values are compared as a

pair and not individually. Both must match for the filter to return TRUE.

If I wanted a listing of order numbers that contained sales of book written by authors that live in Missouri or stores that sold the books in South Carolina, I would use a non-pair-wise comparison.

```
SQL> select
  2     order_number
  3  from sales
  4  where
  5     book_key in (select book_key
  6                   from
  7                     author join book_author
                                using (author_key)
  8                   where author_state = 'MO')
  9  and
 10     store_key  in (select store_key
 12                     from store
 13                     where store_state = 'SC');

ORDER_NUMBER
--------------------
O179
O116
O146
O183
O159
O161
O200
O162
O109

9 rows selected.
```

In this example, I am comparing two columns, but they are unrelated, and so they must be compared in separate filters.

Conclusion

Again, we covered a lot of information in this chapter. We started with sorting and grouping, and then covered table joins and finally ended with subqueries.

SQL joins bring tables together.

Sorting is a major capability of the database; however, it is an expensive operation that should only be used if the results are required to be in a specific order. Large sorts can require heavy disk I/O that can affect the performance of the entire database. Sorts should always be performed last.

Grouping is a type of sorting where the results are sorted into groups based on a designated column. These groups can be passed to a multi-row function. Remember that any column in the SELECT clause must be in the GROUP BY list, but the GROUP BY list may have columns that are not in the SELECT clause.

Table joins are used to relate two or more tables. You have the choice of using the Oracle standard syntax or using ANSI SQL. The advantage of the ANSI SQL format is that all join information is located in the FROM clause, and the WHERE clause is used exclusively for filtering. Tables are joined on common columns.

A Cartesian join returns all possible row combinations, which is usually the result of failing to properly define the join. An outer join returns all the rows from the outer table and the matching rows from the other table, filling the missing columns with NULLs. A full outer join requires that you use the ANSI SQL format, because it is not supported in the Oracle format. The ANSI natural join should be avoided as it makes the query harder to understand and can lead to errors if the underlying tables are changed.

Subqueries are queries within queries. Subqueries are very powerful but also can lead to very complicated queries that perform poorly. Subqueries can be used in all the SQL clauses to include SELECT, FROM, WHERE and HAVING. Single row subqueries use the equal operators and must only return one row. Multi-row subqueries use set operators and can return one or more rows.

Multi-column subqueries can be used for pair-wise comparison of more than one value. If you need a non-pair-wise comparison, you must use a separate filter for each value.

So far we have covered the subjects needed to create complex, powerful queries. In the next chapter, we will begin to put that capability to use. Chapter 4 will include building complex queries and using SQL to manipulate the data in the database.

Oracle Tables And DML

Oracle Tables and DML

In this chapter, we are going to discuss Oracle database tables; how to create and manage them. Tables are the bases for relational database. Other database objects will be introduced in Chapter 5.

Once we have an understanding of Oracle tables and how data is stored in them, we are ready to move to manipulating the data. So far, we have just pulled information from the database. How did that data get there, and how can we change the data already in the database? This is the function of the INSERT, UPDATE and DELETE statements. Together, they are referred to as data manipulation language (DML).

DML vs. DDL

DML changes data in an object. If you insert a row into a table, that is DML. You have manipulated the data. When you create, change or remove a database object, it is referred to as date definition language (DDL). As we will discuss at the end of this chapter, all DDL statements issue an implicit commit, so they are a permanent change. All DML statements change data and must be committed before the change becomes permanent.

Managing Tables

The table is the basic building block of any database system. We discussed tables in Chapter 1 and talked about normalizing data to remove redundancy. In this section, we are going to discuss the different types of tables inside an Oracle database and how they are created and used. We need this information as we progress into manipulating the data in tables with the INSERT, UPDATE and DELETE statements. In computer parlance, updates are DML.

You create a table by defining the column names and their data types. Columns can be any of the data types discussed in Chapter 2, to include user defined data types. When we loaded the PUBS schema, we ran the *pubs_db.sql* script that contained the commands to create the tables. Let's look at the AUTHOR table.

```
CREATE TABLE AUTHOR
(
  AUTHOR_KEY              VARCHAR2(11),
  AUTHOR_LAST_NAME        VARCHAR2(40),
  AUTHOR_FIRST_NAME       VARCHAR2(20),
  AUTHOR_PHONE            VARCHAR2(12),
  AUTHOR_STREET           VARCHAR2(40),
  AUTHOR_CITY             VARCHAR2(20),
  AUTHOR_STATE            VARCHAR2(2),
  AUTHOR_ZIP              VARCHAR2(5),
  AUTHOR_CONTRACT_NBR     NUMBER(5)
);
```

This statement creates a table named AUTHOR that contains nine columns defined within the parentheses. Each column definition is separated by a coma and contains the data type and size of the column. The CREATE TABLE command can be quite involved, defining the table storage location and constraints.

```
CREATE TABLE "PUBS"."EDITOR"
(
  "EDITOR_KEY" VARCHAR2(9) NOT NULL,
  "EDITOR_LAST_NAME" VARCHAR2(30) NOT NULL,
  "EDITOR_FIRST_NAME" VARCHAR2(30) NOT NULL,
  "HIRE_DATE" DATE DEFAULT SYSDATE NOT NULL,
```

```
"EDITOR_ACTIVE" CHAR(1) DEFAULT 'Y',
 CONSTRAINT "EDITOR_PK" PRIMARY KEY("EDITOR_KEY")
    USING INDEX
    TABLESPACE "INDX"
)  TABLESPACE "USERS"
```

In the example above, I created a table called EDITOR in the PUBS schema or user. It has five columns, all of which will not allow NULL values except for *editor_active*. The *hire_date* column will default to the SYSDATE, if a date is not provided when a row is inserted. Likewise, the *editor_active* column will default to Y. I defined a primary key constraint on the *editor_key* called *editor_pk*. The *editor_pk* constraint uses an index, which will be built in the INDX tablespace. The table itself will be built in the USERS tablespace.

Oracle command syntax is complex and precise

We are not going to get that involved with our table creation at this time, since most of those items belong in the realm of the DBA or will be covered in detail in Chapter 5. By default, the table will be created in the user's default tablespace defined when the user was created. Also, columns not defined as NOT NULL will accept NULL values. If I wanted to see my user information, I could query the *user_users* view with this command:

```
SQL> desc user_users;

 Name                                      Null?    Type
 ----------------------------------------- -------- -------------
 USERNAME                                  NOT NULL VARCHAR2(30)
 USER_ID                                   NOT NULL NUMBER
 ACCOUNT_STATUS                            NOT NULL VARCHAR2(32)
 LOCK_DATE                                          DATE
 EXPIRY_DATE                                        DATE
 DEFAULT_TABLESPACE                        NOT NULL VARCHAR2(30)
 TEMPORARY_TABLESPACE                      NOT NULL VARCHAR2(30)
 CREATED                                   NOT NULL DATE
 INITIAL_RSRC_CONSUMER_GROUP                        VARCHAR2(30)
 EXTERNAL_NAME                                      VARCHAR2(4000)

SQL> select default_tablespace from user_users;

DEFAULT_TABLESPACE
------------------------------
USERS
```

Since the user views will only show me information that belongs to me, the *user_users* view will only display my information, since I am the only user defined as me.

Once we have created the table, we can begin inserting data. Sometimes, I want to create a table to hold some data temporarily. This would allow me to temporarily create a table with some intermediate data in it, that I then could repeatedly query from. This is very easy with something called CTAS (pronounced "sea-taz").

Create Table as Select

The boss just had a great idea, let's give an award to all the stores that have above average sales. Of course, we have to determine which stores have above average sales. Let's look at the data we will need to determine this. First, we need to know the average sales for each store. Next, we need to know the average of the average sales by store. Finally, we need to know which stores have average sales that are above the average.

We can easily create a table based on a query and insert the results of the query into the table. We want a list of store names and their average sales, and we will use this data in a number of other queries so let's store it temporarily in a table.

```
SQL> create table t1 as
  2   select
  3     store_name,
  4     avg(quantity) qty
  5   from
  6     store join sales using (store_key)
  7   group by store_name;

Table created.
SQL> desc t1
 Name                                    Null?    Type
 --------------------------------------- -------- ----------------
 STORE_NAME                                       VARCHAR2(40)
 QTY                                              NUMBER
```

The first statement uses the query to create a table. The columns in the query define the new table column definitions and their data types are taken from the original tables. The column avg(quantity) had to be aliased because avg(quantity) is not a valid column name. In this case, I aliased the column to qty. The quantity column in the sales table is defined as NUMBER(5). Because the quantity values were passed through the average function, the database used the default NUMBER as the results data type. A NUMBER is the same as NUMBER(38). By selecting from the T1 table, we can see that the database also inserted all the rows from the query results into the table.

```
SQL> select * from t1;

STORE_NAME                                      QTY
--------------------------------------- ----------
barnes and Noble                                545
blue ride booksellers                           540
books for dummies                        1181B81818
borders                                  1821B66667
eaton books                              1346B66667
hot wet and mushy books                  1452B94118
ignoramus and dufus                       401B111111
quagmire books                                  790
specialty bookstore                      1013B33333
wee bee books                            1141B66667
```

The one command created a new table and loaded it with the requested data. Now, we can use table T1 in our other queries. Let's create another table that contains the average of the qty column in T1.

```
SQL> create table t2 as
  2   select
  3     avg(qty) Average_Sales
  4   from t1;

Table created.

SQL> desc t2
 Name                                      Null?    Type
 ----------------------------------------- -------- --------
 AVERAGE_SALES                                      NUMBER
```

I can now create a query that will give us the store names for stores with above average sales.

```
SQL> select
  2     store_name
  3   from
  4     t1
  5   where qty > (select average_sales from t2);

STORE_NAME
----------------------------------------
books for dummies
borders
eaton books
hot wet and mushy books
wee bee books

5 rows selected.
```

Above is the list of stores with above average sales. This is too good to waste, so let's turn this into a script that we can use over and over again.

```
-- Compute the Stores with above average sales.

set pages 999 line 74

-- create table t1
create table t1 as
```

```
select
  store_name,
  avg(quantity) qty
from
  store join sales using (store_key)
group by store_name;

-- create table t2
create table
    t2
as
select
  avg(qty) Average_Sales
from t1;

--  Create the Report

set feedback off trimspool on

select
   initcap (store_name) "Store Name"
from
   t1
where
   qty > (select average_sales from t2)
order by
   qty;

set pages 999 line 74 feedback on
```

The script works, but when we run it there are errors on the CTAS queries.

```
SQL> @avg_sales
create table t1 as
            *
ERROR at line 1:
ORA-00955: name is already used by an existing object

create table t2 as
            *
ERROR at line 1:
ORA-00955: name is already used by an existing object

Store Name
----------------------------------------
Wee Bee Books
Books For Dummies
Eaton Books
Hot Wet And Mushy Books
Borders
```

The problem is that T1 and T2 are real, permanent tables in the database. To rerun the script, we need to first remove these tables from the database.

DROP/DELETE/TRUNCATE Tables

As we said at the beginning of the chapter, creating a table is DDL. Dropping a table is also a DDL statement, because it modifies an object in the database rather that data in an object.

Each of these commands will either remove the table from the database or remove the rows from the table. If we want to remove the table and all it's data from the database, we use the drop command.

```
SQL> drop table t1;

Table dropped.
```

The DROP command is used to remove any database object from the database. It works by removing the object definition. Since the object no longer exists, it can no longer be used. The drop command is DDL because it defines objects in the database. Anytime you execute a DDL command, you implicitly issue a commit and the statement cannot be rolled back. This is discussed in the last section of this chapter.

The term "dropping" has a different meaning in Oracle

The DELETE command will not remove the table but will remove all the rows in the table.

```
SQL> select count(*) from t1;

  COUNT(*)
----------
        10

1 row selected.

SQL> delete t1;

10 rows deleted.

SQL> rollback;

Rollback complete.

SQL> delete from t1;

10 rows deleted.
```

In this example, there are ten rows in table T1. The DELETE T1 command deletes all ten rows. The DELETE command is a DML command that does not issue an implicit commit. For that reason, I can rollback the DELETE. The DELETE FROM T1 command is the equivalent of the DELETE T1 command and can also be rolled back. We will cover deleting rows in detail later. The rollback command will be covered in the last section of this chapter.

Truncate: A One-Way Trip

So, how do I remove all the rows from a large table quickly? The fastest way is to truncate the table. The TRUNCATE command is also DML, so it also issues an implicit commit and cannot be rolled back. The TRUNCATE command is so fast because it basically resets the table definition to be a new empty table.

The database does not actually delete any rows, but because the table definition is now an empty table, the database has no way to actually retrieve the old rows. As the table begins to grow, the space where the old rows were written gets overwritten with the new rows. The TRUNCATE command can get rid of the data in a very large table quickly and efficiently, as long as you do not need to be able to rollback the delete.

```
SQL> truncate table t1;
Table truncated.
```

Because you cannot recover data from a truncated table, it should be used with caution. You will normally want to delete the rows.

I think I should not have truncated that table!

What we need to do now is update our script to drop the tables T1 and T2.

```
-- Compute the Stores with above average sales.

set pages 999 line 74

-- Clean Up Old Tables
drop table t1;
drop table t2;

-- create table t1
create table t1 as
select
  store_name,
  avg(quantity) qty
from
  store join sales using (store_key)
group by store_name;

-- create table t2
create table t2 as
select
  avg(qty) Average_Sales
from t1;

--  Create the Report

set feedback off trimspool on

select
  initcap (store_name) "Store Name"
from
 t1
where
  qty > (select average_sales from t2)
order by qty;

set pages 999 line 74 feedback on
```

Now, I run my script in SQL*Plus.

```
SQL> @avg_sales

Table dropped.
Table dropped.

Table created.

Table created.
```

```
Store Name
----------------------------------------
Wee Bee Books
Books For Dummies
Eaton Books
Hot Wet And Mushy Books
Borders
```

I did not turn *feedback* off until right before the query ran, because I wanted to demonstrate that the tables were being dropped and recreated. You can remove those notices by setting feedback off at the beginning of the script.

There is overhead to creating tables to hold temporary data. In our script, we create T1 and then query from it twice. The more we reuse T1, the more efficient it is to create the table. If you look at the listing below, you will see that most of the processing time was spent creating and dropping the T1 and T2 tables.

```
SQL> set timing on
SQL> @avg_sales

Table dropped.

Elapsed: 00:00:00.04

Table dropped.

Elapsed: 00:00:00.21

Table created.

Elapsed: 00:00:00.23

Table created.

Elapsed: 00:00:00.01

Store Name
----------------------------------------
Wee Bee Books
Books For Dummies
Eaton Books
Hot Wet And Mushy Books
Borders
Elapsed: 00:00:00.02
```

When you set timing ON, SQL*Plus shows the time spent executing each command. This is database server time; time spent on the server executing the command. Noticed that my script used 0.51 seconds to run, but that .49 of that time was spent creating and dropping the tables. We can rewrite this query using subqueries in place of the tables.

```
SQL> select
  2    initcap (store_name) "Store Name"
  3  from
  4    (select
  5      store_name,
  6      avg(quantity) qty
  7    from
  8      store join sales using (store_key)
  9    group by store_name) a
 10  where qty > (select
 11                    avg(qty) Average_Sales
 12                  from (select
 13                          store_name,
 14                          avg(quantity) qty
 15                        from
 16                          store join sales using (store_key)
 17                        group by store_name))
 18  order by qty;

Store Name
----------------------------------------
Wee Bee Books
Books For Dummies
Eaton Books
Hot Wet And Mushy Books
Borders

5 rows selected.

Elapsed: 00:00:00.00
```

In the example above, I replaced each of the tables holding temporary data with the tables defining query. What I was left with was a query with 3 subqueries, one of which was nested inside a subquery. Looks inefficient, but when I ran the query, it executed faster that .01 seconds. So, before making tables to hold temporary data, insure that you will reuse the data enough to overcome the overhead of dropping and recreating those tables. So far, we have seen two ways to get the same information, stores with above average sales. In SQL, there are many paths to the same answer. Here is another method using the HAVING clause.

```
SQL> select
  2      store_name,
  3      sum(quantity) store_sales,
  4      (select sum(quantity)
  5       from sales)/(select count(*)
  6                    from store) avg_sales
  7  from
  8    store   s,
  9    sales   sl
 10   where
 11      s.store_key = sl.store_key
 12   having
 13      sum(quantity) > (select sum(quantity)
 14                       from sales)/(select count(*)
 15                                    from store)
 16   group by
 17      store_name
  ;

STORE_NAME                               STORE_SALES  AVG_SALES
---------------------------------------- -----------  ----------
books for dummies                              13000       11095
borders                                        21860       11095
eaton books                                    12120       11095
hot wet and sexy books                         24700       11095
wee bee books                                  13700       11095

Elapsed: 00:00:00.00
```

Notice in the example above that the results are the same stores but in a different order. Since we did not order the results, they are listed as the database found them as it accessed the tables. Different access paths return results in different orders.

Finally there is another method that is available with ANSI SQL using the *with* clause. The *with* clause comes at the beginning of the query and is used to create tables in memory that can be used in the query. In Oracle you need to use a SQL hint to insure that the database creates these tables once and uses them over and over again. The query look a bit confusing because you define the *with* clause first. Basically the *with* clause replaces the CTAS.

```
with sumsale as
  (select /*+ materialize */
            sum(quantity) totalsales
   from
     sales)
```

The statement above is the same as:

```
create table sumsale as
select
  sum(quantity) totalsales
from
  sales;
```

You just don't have the overhead of actually creating a physical table in the database.

```
SQL> with sumsale as
  2      (select /*+ materialize */
  3         sum(quantity) totalsales
  4       from sales)
  5  select
  6      store_name,
  7      sum(quantity) store_sales,
  8      (select totalsales from sumsale)/(select count(*)
  9                                        from store) avg_sales
 10  from
 11      store   natural join sales
 12  having
 13      sum(quantity) > (select totalsales
 14                       from sumsale)/(select count(*)
 15                                      from store)
 16  group by
 17      store_name
 18  ;

STORE_NAME                               STORE_SALES  AVG_SALES
---------------------------------------- -----------  ----------
books for dummies                              13000       11055
borders                                        21860       11055
eaton books                                    12120       11055
hot wet and sexy books                         24700       11055
wee bee books                                  13700       11055
```

Notice that we create the *sumsale* table in memory and queried from it twice. The *with* clause is just one of the advanced SQL capabilities that Oracle implements.

Altering Tables: Add Columns

Once we have our tables, we may need to make some changes as our database grows and our data changes. If the table is empty, we normally just drop and recreate it. If the table has data, then we need to modify the table in place with the ALTER TABLE command. Note that the ALTER TABLE command is DML and issues an implicit commit.

Sometimes, we find that a piece of data that we did not maintain becomes important, and we need to add it to the database. We can add a table to hold the new data or add it to our current schema by adding a column to a current table. For example, we discover that we need to keep a record of the last date that each author published and what they published. We need to add two columns to the author table, *author_last_published* (a date) and *author_item_published* (a varchar2(40)). To do this, we use the ALTER TABLE ADD command.

```
SQL> alter table author add (author_last_published  date);

Table altered.

SQL> alter table author add (author_item_published  varchar2(40));

Table altered.

SQL> desc author
 Name                                     Null?     Type
 ---------------------------------------- --------  --------------------
 AUTHOR_KEY                                         VARCHAR2(11)
 AUTHOR_LAST_NAME                                   VARCHAR2(40)
 AUTHOR_FIRST_NAME                                  VARCHAR2(20)
 AUTHOR_PHONE                                       VARCHAR2(12)
 AUTHOR_STREET                                      VARCHAR2(40)
 AUTHOR_CITY                                        VARCHAR2(20)
 AUTHOR_STATE                                       VARCHAR2(2)
 AUTHOR_ZIP                                         VARCHAR2(5)
 AUTHOR_CONTRACT_NBR                                NUMBER(5)
 AUTHOR_LAST_PUBLISHED                              DATE
 AUTHOR_ITEM_PUBLISHED                              VARCHAR2(40)
```

Notice that the new columns are at the end of the AUTHOR table. All current rows in the table now contain NULLs for the new columns.

```
select
  author_key,
  author_last_published,
  author_item_published
from
  author;

AUTHOR_KEY  AUTHOR_LA AUTHOR_ITEM_PUBLISHED
----------- --------- ---------------------------------------
A101
A102
A103
A104
A105
A106
A107
A108
A109
A110

10 rows selected.
```

I added each column separately, but you can add as many columns as needed in one command by separating them with commas.

```
alter table author add (author_last_published  date,
                        author_item_published  varchar2(40));
```

If I define a default value for the new columns, all the current columns will have the default value. (I dropped and recreated the original author table.)

```
SQL> alter table author add (
  2      author_last_published  date default SYSDATE,
  3      author_item_published  varchar2(40)
  4                  default 'Magizine Article' not null
  5  );

Table altered.

select
  author_key,
  author_last_published,
```

```
  author_item_published
from
  author;

SQL>

AUTHOR_KEY  AUTHOR_LA AUTHOR_ITEM_PUBLISHED
----------- --------- ------------------------------------
A101        20-FEB-05 Magizine Article
A102        20-FEB-05 Magizine Article
A103        20-FEB-05 Magizine Article
A104        20-FEB-05 Magizine Article
A105        20-FEB-05 Magizine Article
A106        20-FEB-05 Magizine Article
A107        20-FEB-05 Magizine Article
A108        20-FEB-05 Magizine Article
A109        20-FEB-05 Magizine Article
A110        20-FEB-05 Magizine Article

10 rows selected.
```

Notice that the *author_item_published* column was created not allowing NULL values. I can do this because I specified a default value that was applied to all the current rows before I added the NOT NULL constraint. If I did not define a default value, the ALTER TABLE command would have failed.

```
SQL> alter table author add (
  2      author_last_published  date default SYSDATE,
  3      author_item_published  varchar2(40) not null
  4  );
alter table author add (
            *
ERROR at line 1:
ORA-01758: table must be empty to add mandatory (NOT NULL) column
```

Altering Tables: Drop Columns

Sometimes, you find that you have columns that are not being used. The data no longer is collected or relevant. In this case, you need to remove some columns from your database. With Oracle8i and later, you can remove a column from a table with the ALTER TABLE DROP COLUMN command.

```
SQL> desc author
Name                                   Null?    Type
-------------------------------------- -------- --------------
AUTHOR_KEY                                      VARCHAR2(11)
AUTHOR_LAST_NAME                                VARCHAR2(40)
AUTHOR_FIRST_NAME                               VARCHAR2(20)
AUTHOR_PHONE                                    VARCHAR2(12)
AUTHOR_STREET                                   VARCHAR2(40)
AUTHOR_CITY                                     VARCHAR2(20)
AUTHOR_STATE                                    VARCHAR2(2)
AUTHOR_ZIP                                      VARCHAR2(5)
AUTHOR_CONTRACT_NBR                             NUMBER(5)

SQL> alter table author drop column author_contract_nbr;

Table altered.

SQL> desc author
Name                                   Null?    Type
-------------------------------------- -------- --------------
AUTHOR_KEY                                      VARCHAR2(11)
AUTHOR_LAST_NAME                                VARCHAR2(40)
AUTHOR_FIRST_NAME                               VARCHAR2(20)
AUTHOR_PHONE                                    VARCHAR2(12)
AUTHOR_STREET                                   VARCHAR2(40)
AUTHOR_CITY                                     VARCHAR2(20)
AUTHOR_STATE                                    VARCHAR2(2)
AUTHOR_ZIP                                      VARCHAR2(5)
```

If the column you dropped had an index or a constraint defined on it, those objects would also be dropped. If the column is part of a multicolumn constraint, you must use "cascade constraint" in the ALTER TABLE command and the entire constraint is also dropped.

```
SQL> alter table author
  2   drop column author_contract_nbr cascade constraint;

Table altered.
```

Dropping a column can be a time and resource consuming operation if the table is large. As an alternative to dropping a column, you can set the column as unused. The column actually stays in the table, but the database does not allow access to it. Later, when you have a maintenance period, you can drop the unused columns.

```
SQL> desc author
 Name                                      Null?    Type
 ----------------------------------------- -------- ----------------
 AUTHOR_KEY                                          VARCHAR2(11)
 AUTHOR_LAST_NAME                                    VARCHAR2(40)
 AUTHOR_FIRST_NAME                                   VARCHAR2(20)
 AUTHOR_PHONE                                        VARCHAR2(12)
 AUTHOR_STREET                                       VARCHAR2(40)
 AUTHOR_CITY                                         VARCHAR2(20)
 AUTHOR_STATE                                        VARCHAR2(2)
 AUTHOR_ZIP                                          VARCHAR2(5)
 AUTHOR_CONTRACT_NBR                                 NUMBER(5)

SQL> alter table author set unused column author_first_name;

Table altered.

SQL> desc author
 Name                                      Null?    Type
 ----------------------------------------- -------- ----------------
 AUTHOR_KEY                                          VARCHAR2(11)
 AUTHOR_LAST_NAME                                    VARCHAR2(40)
 AUTHOR_PHONE                                        VARCHAR2(12)
 AUTHOR_STREET                                       VARCHAR2(40)
 AUTHOR_CITY                                         VARCHAR2(20)
 AUTHOR_STATE                                        VARCHAR2(2)
 AUTHOR_ZIP                                          VARCHAR2(5)
 AUTHOR_CONTRACT_NBR                                 NUMBER(5)

SQL> select * from user_unused_col_tabs;

TABLE_NAME                        COUNT
------------------------------   ----------
AUTHOR                                1

1 row selected.

SQL> alter table author drop unused columns;

Table altered.

SQL> select * from user_unused_col_tabs;

no rows selected
```

In the example above, I marked the *author_contract_nbr* column as
unused. Once marked unused, the command cannot be rolled
back. The column is gone for all practical purposes. The cleanup
is delayed until the DROP UNUSED COLUMNS command is
issued. There is a view, called the *user_unused_col_tabs* view that
contains the table name and the number of columns marked
unused. In the example above it, the AUTHOR table contained

one unused column. Once I dropped the unused columns, the view was empty.

Altering Tables: Modifying Columns

You can make some modifications to columns, if needed. Basically, any column can grow. Any column can shrink if it does not contain data larger than the new size, but only empty columns can change data types. Columns are modified using the ALTER TABLE MODIFY command.

```
SQL> desc author
 Name                                      Null?    Type
 ----------------------------------------- -------- --------------
 AUTHOR_KEY                                          VARCHAR2(11)
 AUTHOR_LAST_NAME                                    VARCHAR2(40)
 AUTHOR_FIRST_NAME                                   VARCHAR2(20)
 AUTHOR_PHONE                                        VARCHAR2(12)
 AUTHOR_STREET                                       VARCHAR2(40)
 AUTHOR_CITY                                         VARCHAR2(20)
 AUTHOR_STATE                                        VARCHAR2(2)
 AUTHOR_ZIP                                          VARCHAR2(5)
 AUTHOR_CONTRACT_NBR                                 NUMBER(5)

SQL> alter table author modify
  2  (
  3     author_last_name varchar2(80),
  4     author_first_name varchar2(15)
  5  );

Table altered.

SQL> desc author
 Name                                      Null?    Type
 ----------------------------------------- -------- --------------
 AUTHOR_KEY                                          VARCHAR2(11)
 AUTHOR_LAST_NAME                                    VARCHAR2(80)
 AUTHOR_FIRST_NAME                                   VARCHAR2(15)
 AUTHOR_PHONE                                        VARCHAR2(12)
 AUTHOR_STREET                                       VARCHAR2(40)
 AUTHOR_CITY                                         VARCHAR2(20)
 AUTHOR_STATE                                        VARCHAR2(2)
 AUTHOR_ZIP                                          VARCHAR2(5)
 AUTHOR_CONTRACT_NBR                                 NUMBER(5)
```

In the example above, we extended the size of *author_last_name* to 80 characters and reduced the size of *author_first_name* to 15 characters. If we try to reduce *author_first_name* smaller than the largest name in the table, the command will fail.

```
SQL> alter table author modify (author_first_name varchar2(5));
alter table author modify (author_first_name varchar2(5))
                            *
ERROR at line 1:
ORA-01441: cannot decrease column length because some value is too
big
```

All data in the database is stored in tables, and so far we have covered in detail how to retrieve the data from a table. In this chapter, we talked about creating and maintaining tables. Now it is time to cover putting data into tables and changing the data already in tables. This is referred to as data manipulation and involves the INSERT, UPDATE and DELETE statements. We want to start with getting the data into the table, so we start with the INSERT statement.

INSERT

In all the examples in this book, we have been pulling data from the PUBS schema which was loaded using the *pubs_db.sql* script in the code depot. This script created all our tables and loaded all the practice data. To load the data in the tables, it used the INSERT statement. Below are a few lines from the script loading data into the *book_author* table.

```
--*****************************************
-- Insert book_author (25 rows)
--*****************************************
INSERT INTO BOOK_AUTHOR VALUES ('A101', 'B101', .11);
INSERT INTO BOOK_AUTHOR VALUES ('A102', 'B101', .08);
INSERT INTO BOOK_AUTHOR VALUES ('A103', 'B102', .12);
INSERT INTO BOOK_AUTHOR VALUES ('A104', 'B102', .15);
INSERT INTO BOOK_AUTHOR VALUES ('A105', 'B103', .10);
INSERT INTO BOOK_AUTHOR VALUES ('A109', 'B104', .12);
INSERT INTO BOOK_AUTHOR VALUES ('A110', 'B105', .13);
INSERT INTO BOOK_AUTHOR VALUES ('A104', 'B106', .16);
```

Each statement loads one row of data. The basic statement is:

```
insert into <table name> (col1, col2, col3,…)
                    values (val1, val2, val3,…);
```

If the values listed are in the same order as the table columns and there is a value (even if it is NULL) for each column, you can leave out the column list as in the example above. The easiest way to determine which columns are in the table is to describe the table (SQL> desc author) as we have been doing in our examples. If you exclude a column from the INSERT, then the column list is mandatory because the database needs to match the values to the columns. Excluded columns will contain NULL unless the table has a default value defined for that column. First, let's insert a new row in the SALES table.

```
SQL> insert into sales values (
  2     'S124',
  3     'B124',
  4     'O504',
  5     to_date ('01-02-2005 14:30','MM-DD-YYYY HH24:MI'),
  6     100);

1 row created.
```

This INSERT statement has a value for each column, and they are ordered the same as the table.

```
SQL> insert into sales values ('S120','B120','O500',100);
insert into sales values ('S120','B120','O500',100)
                                                *
ERROR at line 1:
ORA-00947: not enough values
```

Here, we left out the order date, and the database rejected the row.

```
SQL> insert into sales
  2  (store_key, book_key, order_number, quantity)
  3  values
  4  ('S121',    'B121',   'O501',       100);

1 row created.
```

In the example above, we do not have the order date but we listed the columns that for which we have values. In this case, the order date is NULL.

```
SQL> insert into sales values ('S122','B122','O502',NULL,100);

1 row created.
```

Here, we are also missing the order date, but we included the NULL in our values list. Since there are the correct number and type of values, the database inserted the row.

```
SQL> insert into sales values ('S123','B123',503,NULL,100);

1 row created.
```

The above example demonstrates that if you provide bad data, but of the correct number and type, the database will insert the row. In example above, the order number is a number (503) rather than a varchar2. The database implicitly converted 503 to "503" and inserted the row. Since this is an invalid order number (all order numbers start with 'O'), we have bad data in the database. In the end, here are the rows inserted in the examples above.

```
SQL> select * from sales;

STOR BOOK_K ORDER_NUMBER         ORDER_DAT  QUANTITY
---- ------ -------------------- ---------  ----------
S124 B124   O504                 02-JAN-05       100
S121 B121   O501                                 100
S122 B122   O502                                 100
S123 B123   503                                  100
S101 B101   O101                 02-JAN-04      1000
...
```

The missing dates are NULL, and order number 503 has a bad order number.

I can also insert data using a query. The principle is the same as creating a table with CTAS, except that you must already have the table. Here, I create table T5.

```
create table t5
(
  k_book   varchar2(9),
  k_store  varchar2(9),
  k_order  varchar2(9)
);
```

Now, I insert the data that I get from the SALES table. I query the same columns (even if they have different names) from the SALES table. Notice that when you use a query to insert data, the values parameter is not use in the INSERT statement.

```
SQL> insert into t5
  2   select
  3     book_key,
  4     store_key,
  5     order_number
  6   from sales;

104 rows created.
```

If I query the columns in a different order, I must have a column list to define the order.

```
SQL> insert into t5 (k_store, k_order, k_book)
  2   select
  3     store_key,
  4     order_number,
  5     book_key
  6   from sales;

104 rows created.
```

Remember that the INSERT statement must be able to determine which values are being inserted into which columns or it will reject the data.

Now that we have our data in the table, how do we change it? The UPDATE statement is used to change data already in the table.

UPDATE

The UPDATE statement locates one or more rows (or all the rows) in a table and sets one or more columns to the specified values. As with the INSERT statement, the values must either match the columns data type or one that the database can implicitly convert. The basic format is:

```
update <table name> set (<col1 = val1, col2 = val2,col3 = val3,…)
   where <expression identifying rows to change>;
```

Let's go back to the AUTHOR table and look at some examples of updates. As with the INSERT section, I rolled back the changes to the original table.

To set each author contract number to zero, simply leave off the WHERE clause. If you do not specify a row, then all rows are updated.

```
SQL> select author_key, author_contract_nbr from author;

AUTHOR_KEY   AUTHOR_CONTRACT_NBR
----------   -------------------
A101                        5601
A102                        5602
A103                        5603
A104                        6602
A105                        7896
A106                        6547
A107                        3452
A108                        7954
A109                           1
A110                        2853

10 rows selected.

SQL> update author set author_contract_nbr = 0000;

10 rows updated.
```

```
SQL> select author_key, author_contract_nbr from author;

AUTHOR_KEY   AUTHOR_CONTRACT_NBR
-----------  --------------------
A101                            0
A102                            0
A103                            0
A104                            0
A105                            0
A106                            0
A107                            0
A108                            0
A109                            0
A110                            0

10 rows selected.

SQL> rollback;
```

The ROLLBACK command returns the table to the state it was in before the updates.

To change the contract number for author A109 to 999, use the statement below. Notice that the WHERE clause identifies which row to update.

```
SQL> update
  2     author
  3   set author_contract_nbr = 999
  4   where
  5     author_key = 'A109';

1 row updated.

SQL> select author_key, author_contract_nbr from author;

AUTHOR_KEY   AUTHOR_CONTRACT_NBR
-----------  --------------------
A101                         5601
A102                         5602
A103                         5603
A104                         6602
A105                         7896
A106                         6547
A107                         3452
A108                         7954
A109                          999
A110                         2853

10 rows selected.
```

I can also set multiple columns in one update. A comma separates each column to be changed. All of the columns identified will be changed for all the rows specified in the WHERE clause.

```
SQL> update
  2    author
  3  set author_contract_nbr = 8888,
  4      author_zip          = 32076
  5  where
  6    author_state = 'MO';

3 rows updated.

SQL> select
  2    author_key,
  3    author_state,
  4    author_zip,
  4    author_contract_nbr
  6  from
  7    author;

AUTHOR_KEY  AU AUTHO AUTHOR_CONTRACT_NBR
----------- -- ----- -------------------
A101        MO 32076                8888
A102        MO 32076                8888
A103        MO 32076                8888
A104        CA 91607                6602
A105        IL 57307                7896
A106        TX 77304                6547
A107        WI 33301                3452
A108        KY 45461                7954
A109        LA 47301                   1
A110        MA 47301                2853

10 rows selected.
```

One of the powerful features of the update statement is the ability to update rows using a query.

```
update <table name> set (col1, col2, col3,…) = (<query>)
   where <expression>;
```

The query must have a value in the select clause for each column in the column list. If the where clause is not used all rows are updated.

```
SQL> update
  2      sales
  3   set (order_date, quantity) = (select
  4                                      SYSDATE,
  5                                      avg(quantity)
  6                                  from sales
  7                                  where book_key = 'B102'
  8                                  group by book_key, SYSDATE)
  9   where book_key = 'B102';

11 rows updated.
```

Here, we modify the SALES tables by setting those rows where
the *book_key* is B102 with the order date to the current date, and
the quantity to the average quantity of all orders for book B102.

```
SQL> select
  2      book_key,
  3      order_date,
  4      quantity
  5   from sales
  6   where book_key in ('B101','B102');

BOOK_K ORDER_DAT   QUANTITY
------ ---------  ----------
B101   02-JAN-04      1000
B102   21-FEB-05      1481
B102   21-FEB-05      1481
B102   21-FEB-05      1481
B102   21-FEB-05      1481
B102   21-FEB-05      1481
B102   21-FEB-05      1481
B101   12-FEB-04       100
B102   21-FEB-05      1481
B102   21-FEB-05      1481
B102   21-FEB-05      1481
B101   02-APR-04       300
B102   21-FEB-05      1481
B101   17-MAY-04      8000
B102   21-FEB-05      1481
B101   20-MAY-04      8800
```

The query in the UPDATE statement defines the values to update the
columns. I still needed the WHERE clause in the UPDATE statement to
define which rows were to be updated.

So far, we can insert new rows, change rows already in the table, and now we need a way to remove rows that we no longer want in the table.

I think I forgot the WHERE clause on that UPDATE!

DELETE

Like the UPDATE statement, the DELETE statement removes all rows identified by the WHERE clause. This is another data manipulation command, which means that we can roll back the deleted data, and that to make our changes permanent, we need to issue a commit. We have already looked at a couple of the DELETE formats.

```
SQL> delete from author;

10 rows deleted.

SQL> rollback;

Rollback complete.

SQL> delete author;

10 rows deleted.

SQL> rollback;

Rollback complete.
```

Both commands deleted all the rows in the table. You cannot delete part of a row. If you want to remove some of the data such as setting all columns to NULL except the *author_key*, you would use the UPDATE statement. The basic format of the command is:

```
delete from <table name> where <expression>;
```

Every row that matches the expression will be removed from the table.

```
SQL> delete from author
  2  where
  3    author_key in ('A101','A103','A120');

2 rows deleted.

SQL> select author_key from author;

AUTHOR_KEY
-----------
A102
A104
A105
A106
A107
A108
A109
A110

8 rows selected.
```

Notice that there is no author with an *author_key* = A120, so only two authors were deleted.

Let's delete the order with the smallest quantity.

```
SQL> delete from sales
  2  where
  3    quantity = (select
  4                   min(quantity)
  5                from
  6                   sales);

1 row deleted.
```

Any valid WHERE clause is acceptable to identify which rows to delete. I can get the same results as above using a nested query and the order number.

```
SQL> delete from sales
  2  where
  3    order_number = (select
  4                          order_number
  5                        from sales
  6                        where quantity = (select
  7                                                min(quantity)
  8                                             from
  9                                                sales));

1 row deleted.
```

But, what happens when I run the above query again?

```
SQL> delete from sales
  2  where
  3    order_number = (select
  4                          order_number
  5                        from sales
  6                        where quantity = (select
  7                                                min(quantity)
  8                                             from
  9                                                sales));
    order_number = (select
                     *
ERROR at line 3:
ORA-01427: single-row subquery returns more than one row
```

What happened? Well, the first time I ran the query, it returned one row because there was only one order number that had the minimum quantity. That order had been deleted. Now, there are many orders that have the new minimum quantity and the query fails. This is an example of writing a query expecting one row, testing it and it working, but then having it fail in other tests. How do I fix it? Change the equals to IN.

```
SQL> delete from sales
  2  where
  3    order_number in (select
  4                          order_number
  5                        from sales
  6                        where quantity = (select
  7                                                min(quantity)
```

```
    8                                  from
    9                                       sales));
47 rows deleted.
```

There were 47 order numbers with the new minimum quantity.

What happens if we rerun the *pubs_db.sql* script while logged on as the PUBS user? The DROP USER command fails (you can't drop yourself while logged on), the CREATE TABLE commands fail (the tables already exist), but the INSERT commands all succeed. Now, we have duplicate rows. We can use the author key to remove the duplicate rows in the author table.

```
SQL> select author_key from author;

AUTHOR_KEY
-----------
A101
A102
A103
A104
A105
A106
A107
A108
A109
A110
A101
A102
A103
A104
A105
A106
A107
A108
A109
A110

20 rows selected.
```

I want to keep one row for each author key. My method is to select all the rows, group them by *author_keys*, select the largest rowid from each group (this is the last inserted row for each author key), and delete the rest.

```
SQL> delete from author
  2  where rowid not in (select
  3                          max(rowid)
  4                      from author
  5                      group by author_key);

10 rows deleted.

SQL> select author_key from author;

AUTHOR_KEY
----------
A101
A102
A103
A104
A105
A106
A107
A108
A109
A110

10 rows selected.
```

This query leaves only the last inserted row for each author key.

Throughout the discussion of INSERTs, UPDATEs and DELETEs, we have seen the ROLLBACK command used to undo the changes. The ROLLBACK command is part of how any database management system implements transactions.

Transactions

A transaction is a logically grouped set of INSERTs, UPDATEs and DELETEs that should all succeed or fail as a group. We just found a new author that has already written a book. We want to enter the data into our PUBS database. Because we normalized our schema, we have to enter the data into three different tables; author, *book_author* and book. We want all three inserts to either succeed or fail as a group; otherwise, we will have some data in some tables but not a complete record of the new author and his book. We log onto the database and insert the three rows of data.

```
SQL> INSERT INTO AUTHOR
  2   VALUES ('A111', 'john',
  3          'garmany', '123-345-4567',
  4          '1234 here st', 'denver',
  5          'CO','90204', '9999');

1 row created.

SQL> INSERT INTO BOOK_AUTHOR VALUES ('A111', 'B130', .20);

1 row created.

SQL> INSERT INTO BOOK
  2   VALUES ('B130', 'P002', 'easy oracle sql',
  3          'miscellaneous', 9.95, 1000, 15, 0, '',
  4          to_date ('02-20-2005','MM-DD-YYYY'));

1 row created.

SQL> commit;

Commit complete.
```

All three of my SQL statements succeeded, so I committed the changes. Once I commit the changes, they are permanently changed in the database and the change cannot be undone. Let's say that one of the three inserts failed. Since I don't want half the information in the database, I can issue a ROLLBACK command and the changes since the last commit (or since log on) are removed from the database and the original state is recreated.

A database transaction is all the changes that take place between a commit or rollback; beginning with the first SQL statement and ending with the subsequent commit or rollback. A commit can be issued as a command or happen because of another statement. Anytime we execute a data definition language (DDL) command, we issue an implicit commit. In the example below, I INSERT a duplicate row with the author key A111. I then create a table (DDL) and rollback.

```
SQL> insert into book_author values ('A111', 'B130', .20);

1 row created.

SQL> create table t1 as
  2   select
  3     store_name,
  4     avg(quantity) qty
from
  5   6     store join sales using (store_key)
  7   group by store_name;

Table created.

SQL> rollback;

Rollback complete.

SQL> select author_key from book_author;

AUTHOR_KEY
-----------
A111
A111
A101
A102
A103
A104
...
A101
A109

27 rows selected.
```

Notice that the duplicate row remains after the rollback. That is because I created a table that issued an implicit commit. The duplicate row was committed by the CREATE TABLE command.

Before a commit or rollback is executed, I have the ability to recover any data changes in the transaction. If I select data that I have changed but not committed, I will get back the changed data. If another user selects data that I have changed but not committed, they will see the original data (a consistent view will be discussed next).

A commit is issued when the user commits, when any DDL statement is executed, or when the user logs off normally. If you make a number of changes and you do not want the changes to be permanent, you must issue a rollback before you log off. Logging off commits the changes.

True story

A user wanted to change a rate for one department. He created and ran his update statement, but he did not use a WHERE clause to limit the changes to the one department. All rows where changed. He realized his mistake, knowing that he did not want to commit the incorrect changes; he instead logged off to go get the DBA to help him. His log off committed the bad data and the company had to restore the previous night's backup and recover the database forward to a time before the user made his changes.

A rollback is issued whenever a user issues the rollback command, abnormally exits the database or the database crashes.

Once a commit has been issued, all changes are permanent. The previous state of the data is permanently lost. Other users will see the committed changes.

Once a rollback has been issued, the changes are undone back to the last commit, rollback or log on. All of the changes are lost (no roll forward).

SAVEPOINT

A SAVEPOINT is a marker within a transaction that allows for a partial rollback. As changes are made in a transaction, we can create SAVEPOINTs to mark different points within the transaction. If we encounter an error, we can rollback to a

SAVEPOINT or all the way back to the beginning of the transaction.

```
SQL> INSERT INTO AUTHOR
  2   VALUES ('A111', 'john',
  3          'garmany', '123-345-4567',
  4          '1234 here st', 'denver',
  5          'CO','90204', '9999');

1 row created.

SQL> savepoint in_author;

Savepoint created.

SQL> INSERT INTO BOOK_AUTHOR VALUES ('A111', 'B130', .20);

1 row created.

SQL> savepoint in_book_author;

Savepoint created.

SQL> INSERT INTO BOOK
  2   VALUES ('B130', 'P002', 'easy oracle sql',
  3          'miscellaneous', 9.95, 1000, 15, 0, '',
  4          to_date ('02-20-2005','MM-DD-YYYY'));

1 row created.

SQL> rollback to in_author;

Rollback complete.
```

In the example above, I inserted a row into the AUTHOR table and created a SAVEPOINT called *in_author*. Next, I inserted a row into the *book_author* table and created another SAVEPOINT called *in_book_author*. Finally, I inserted a row in the BOOK table. I then issued a ROLLBACK to *in_author*. At this point, the row inserted into the AUTHOR table is still there and not committed. The rows added to the book and *book_author* tables have been discarded. At this point, I can continue to make changes, issue a ROLLBACK to the start of the transaction, or issue a COMMIT and commit the row in the author table.

Consistent View

Every database implements some type of consistent view, and how it works is different for each database product. Here, of course, we are going to discuss Oracle's implementation of a consistent view.

In Oracle, a consistent view means that you will never see other users' uncommitted data, otherwise known as a dirty read. If I log onto the database as PUBS and then open a new window and log on again as PUBS, I will have two database sessions, both with user PUBS. Each session is a separate connection, and neither one will be able to see the others' uncommitted data.

Here, I am using the SQL*Plus command SQLPLOMPT to change my prompt, so that you can see the two different users, PUBS1 and PUBS2.

```
SQL> set sqlprompt 'PUBS1 SQL> '
PUBS1 SQL> select author_key from author;

AUTHOR_KEY
----------
A101
A102
A103
A104
A105
A106
A107
A108
A109
A110

10 rows selected.
```

The second PUBS log on sees the same data.

```
PUBS2 SQL> select author_key from author;
```

```
AUTHOR_KEY
-----------
A101
A102
A103
A104
A105
A106
A107
A108
A109
A110

10 rows selected.
```

Now, I add ten additional rows to the AUTHOR table as PUBS1 (I used the INSERT statements from the pubs_db.sql).

```
PUBS1 SQL> INSERT INTO AUTHOR
  2  VALUES ('A101', 'jones', 'mark', '303-462-1222', '1401 west
fourth st', 'st. louis', 'MO','47301', '5601');

1 row created.

PUBS1 SQL> INSERT INTO AUTHOR
  2  VALUES ('A102', 'hester', 'alvis', '523-882-1987', '2503 backer
view st', 'st. louis', 'MO','47301', '5602');

1 row created.

PUBS1 SQL> INSERT INTO AUTHOR
  2  VALUES ('A103', 'weaton', 'erin', '367-980-8622', '6782 hard
day dr', 'st. louis', 'MO','47301', '5603');

1 row created.

PUBS1 SQL> INSERT INTO AUTHOR
  2  VALUES ('A104', 'jeckle', 'pierre', '543-333-9241', '3671 old
fort st', 'north hollywood', 'CA','91607', '6602');

1 row created.

PUBS1 SQL> INSERT INTO AUTHOR
  2  VALUES ('A105', 'withers', 'lester', '457-882-2642', '1320
leaning tree ln', 'pie town', 'IL','57307', '7896');

1 row created.

PUBS1 SQL> INSERT INTO AUTHOR
  2  VALUES ('A106', 'petty', 'juan', '344-455-6572', '8869 wide
creek rd', 'happyville', 'TX','77304', '6547');

1 row created.
```

```
PUBS1 SQL> INSERT INTO AUTHOR
  2   VALUES ('A107', 'clark', 'louis', '666-555-8822', '7980 shallow
pond st', 'rose garden', 'WI','33301', '3452');

1 row created.

PUBS1 SQL> INSERT INTO AUTHOR
  2   VALUES ('A108', 'mee', 'minnie', '321-543-9876', '2356 empty
box rd', 'belaire', 'KY','45461', '7954');

1 row created.

PUBS1 SQL> INSERT INTO AUTHOR
  2   VALUES ('A109', 'shagger', 'dirk', '987-654-3210', '3452 dirt
path way', 'cross trax', 'LA','47301', '0001');

1 row created.

PUBS1 SQL> INSERT INTO AUTHOR
  2   VALUES ('A110', 'smith', 'diego', '564-897-3201', '2567 south
north st', 'tweedle', 'MA','47301', '2853');

1 row created.
```

Now, when PUBS1 checks the AUTHOR table he sees his changes. When PUBS2 checks the AUTHOR table, he still sees only the original ten rows. Remember PUBS1 has not committed the inserts.

```
PUBS1 SQL> select author_key from author;
AUTHOR_KEY
-----------
A101
A102
A103
A104
A105
A106
A107
A108
A109
A110
A101
A102
A103
A104
A105
A106
A107
A108
A109
A110
20 rows selected.
```

```
PUBS2 SQL> select author_key from author;

AUTHOR_KEY
-----------
A101
A102
A103
A104
A105
A106
A107
A108
A109
A110
10 rows selected.
```

Now, PUBS1 commits the changes, and both can now see all 20 rows.

```
PUBS1 SQL> commit;

Commit complete.

PUBS2 SQL> select author_key from author;

AUTHOR_KEY
-----------
A101
A102
A103
A104
A105
A106
A107
A108
A109
A110
A101
A102
A103
A104
A105
A106
A107
A108
A109
A110

20 rows selected.
```

So, what happens when more than one person updates the same data? To get back to the original data, I dropped the AUTHOR table and recreated it from the *pubs_db.sql* script.

First PUBS1 changes the data in the AUTHOR table for key A101.

```
PUBS1 SQL> update author
  2   set author_state = 'CO'
  3   where author_key = 'A101';

1 row updated.

PUBS1 SQL> select author_key, author_state from author;

AUTHOR_KEY  AU
----------  --
A101        CO
A102        MO
A103        MO
A104        CA
A105        IL
A106        TX
A107        WI
A108        KY
A109        LA
A110        MA

10 rows selected.
```

Now it is PUBS2's turn.

```
PUBS2 SQL> update author
  2   set author_state = 'FL'
  3   where author_key = 'A101';
```

The prompt does not come back. That is because PUBS1 has a lock on that data. PUBS2 is waiting behind that lock to change the data. Let's commit PUBS1, so that he releases the lock.

```
PUBS1 SQL> commit;
Commit complete.

PUBS2 SQL> update author
  2   set author_state = 'FL'
  3   where author_key = 'A101';
1 row updated.
```

Once PUBS1 committed, the lock was released and PUBS2 updated the row. Now let's check that consistent view.

```
PUBS1 SQL> select author_key, author_state from author;

AUTHOR_KEY   AU
----------   --
A101         CO
A102         MO
A103         MO
A104         CA
A105         IL
A106         TX
A107         WI
A108         KY
A109         LA
A110         MA

10 rows selected.

PUBS2 SQL> select author_key, author_state from author;

AUTHOR_KEY   AU
----------   --
A101         FL
A102         MO
A103         MO
A104         CA
A105         IL
A106         TX
A107         WI
A108         KY
A109         LA
A110         MA

10 rows selected.
```

PUBS1 sees his committed state of CO, while PUBS2 sees his uncommitted FL. Once PUBS2 commits, both will see FL. PUBS2 overwrote PUBS1. He who commits last wins!

Why did PUBS2's UPDATE end up waiting for the lock held by PUBS1, but the SELECT by PUBS1 did not wait for the lock held by PUBS2? The Oracle database has very loose locking in that it only locks what it has to in order to protect transactions. Locks never block reads. So PUBS1's lock held up PUBS2's

UPDATE of the same piece of data, but it never blocked the SELECT statement that only reads the data.

Somebody's got a lock on my data!

You can sum up Oracle's consistent view in two statements: You will see only committed data and your changes. No user will ever see anyone else's uncommitted data.

Conclusion

We started this chapter with a discussion concerning creating tables. We talked about dropping tables and three methods to remove all the rows from a table: DELTE TABLE; DELETE FROM TABLE; and TRUNCATE table. A key point to remember when creating tables is that the command is a data definition language command (DDL) and thus issues an implicit commit. As we learned later, this makes all changes since the last commit permanent. Remember, CTAS implicitly commits! You can also modify your table by adding, dropping and modifying table columns. Remember that you cannot make a column smaller than the largest value in that column.

We next move to the INSERT, UPDATE, and DELETE statement. Each INSERT creates a new row in the table and any undefined columns are NULLs. The column list is not required if all columns are accounted for in the values list.

All three of the statements can use queries to define values or restrict rows in the WHERE clause.

When using a query, in the UPDATE statement you must insure that each column in the column list has a corresponding value in the query's SELECT clause.

The DELETE statement removes an entire row from the table. All three of the statements are data manipulation language (DML) requiring a COMMIT to make the changes permanent.

Lastly, we covered transactions and Oracle's consistent view. A transaction is a group of statements that are committed or rolled back together. A transaction starts at the last COMMIT or logon and ends at a COMMIT or ROLLBACK. You can partially rollback a transaction if you create SAVEPOINTS. Any DDL issues an implicit commit, ending the current transaction. Oracle's consistent view insures that no user sees any other user's uncommitted data.

In the next chapter, we are going to cover creating and managing database objects such as indexes, constraints, users and views.

Database Objects

If I could figure out which one of these is the database
I could add those objects!

Database Objects

Everything in an Oracle database is an object, from tables to queries. In the last chapter, we introduced you to creating and managing tables; however, there are many other objects in the database. In this chapter, we are going to extend your knowledge of tables by integrating constraints. Constraints protect your data and include primary and foreign keys. They enforce uniqueness and check data before inserting it into a table. We will then discuss views and materialized views, and how they differ from tables and when they are used. Next, we will show you how to use indexes to make your queries more efficient.

All of these objects play an important part in protecting your data, while enhancing the database's efficiency. Let's start our discussion in the last chapter on tables, with some details on integrity constraints.

Integrity Constraints

Constraints protect the integrity of your data. Most DBAs look at constraints as rules attached to a table; however, they are separate objects within the database. They are applied whenever data is added or changed in a table or when the constraint is enabled. Since they are separate objects, they can be disabled or enabled individually. When a constraint is disabled, it remains in the database but is not used to validate data, allowing possibly invalid data to be placed in the table. Some constraints are used to insure that the tables can be related on keys.

Primary Keys

In Chapter 1, we briefly discussed normalization and schema design. One tenet of a normalized design was that each table would have a key and that all of the data in that table would be dependent only on that key. That key is called the primary key for that table. Each table can have only one primary key; however, that key may consist of more than one column. If we look at the AUTHOR table, the *author_key* is the primary key as all the other data in the row relates to only one author key.

I can have two authors named Sam Smith, but I can only have one author key A101. My two Sam Smith authors would each have a unique author key, which would distinguish between them. Although we have been using the author key to join the AUTHOR table to other tables, we do not have a primary key constraint on the table. I can enter a row with a duplicate key, so

my data is not protected. Most primary keys are created as part
of the CREATE TABLE command. But, I can modify my table
to add the primary key if the table already exists.

```
SQL> alter table author
  2>    add (constraint author_pk primary key (author_key));

Table altered.

SQL> desc author
 Name                                      Null?     Type
 ----------------------------------------- -------- ----------------
 AUTHOR_KEY                                NOT NULL VARCHAR2(11)
 AUTHOR_LAST_NAME                                   VARCHAR2(40)
 AUTHOR_FIRST_NAME                                  VARCHAR2(20)
 AUTHOR_PHONE                                       VARCHAR2(12)
 AUTHOR_STREET                                      VARCHAR2(40)
 AUTHOR_CITY                                        VARCHAR2(20)
 AUTHOR_STATE                                       VARCHAR2(2)
 AUTHOR_ZIP                                         VARCHAR2(5)
 AUTHOR_CONTRACT_NBR                                NUMBER(5)
```

Notice that my author key is now listed with a NOT NULL
constraint. That is part of being a primary key. In fact, a primary
key constraint insures that the column (or columns) are not
NULL and are unique. Not allowing NULLs ensures that each
row has an author key. Being unique ensures that no two rows
have the same author key. As we will learn when we discuss
unique constraints, uniqueness is enforced using an index. If we
check for indexes on the author table, we will now find one.

```
SQL> select
  2    index_name,
  3    table_name
  4  from user_indexes;

INDEX_NAME                         TABLE_NAME
---------------------------------- ----------------------------
AUTHOR_PK                          AUTHOR

SQL> select
  2    constraint_name,
  3    constraint_type,
  4    table_name
  5  from user_constraints;
```

```
CONSTRAINT_NAME               C TABLE_NAME
----------------------------- - -------------------------
AUTHOR_PK                     P AUTHOR
```

We now have two additional objects in the database, an index named *author_pk* and a constraint named *author_pk*. Primary keys are normally defined, then you create the table.

```
SQL> create table editor
  2  (
  3    editor_key                varchar2(9) not null,
  4    editor_last_name          varchar2(40),
  5    editor_first_name         varchar2(30),
  6    editor_hire_date          date,
  7    editor_active             char(1)
  8      constraint active_ck check (editor_active in ('Y','N')),
  9    constraint editor_pk primary key (editor_key)
 10      using index tablespace indx
 11  );

Table created.
```

Here, I created a table called EDITOR with a primary key on the *editor_key* column. The index used to enforce the primary key will be built in the *indx* tablespace. If the *"using index tablespace indx"* part is not present, the database creates the index in the user's default tablespace. The primary key is tied directly to the table it is built on. If I drop the table, the constraint is also dropped. I can drop the primary key, however, without dropping the table.

```
SQL> alter table editor drop primary key;

Table altered.

SQL> alter table author disable primary key;

Table altered.

SQL> alter table author enable primary key;

Table altered.
```

In the example above, we dropped the primary key from the EDITOR table. The table remains but the constraint is removed from the database. If we want to have the primary key back, we must recreate it. In the second statement, we disabled the primary key. The key remains in the database but is no longer applied to INSERTSs and UPDATEs. In the last statement, we enabled the key. Dropping or disabling a primary key will cause the database to drop the enforcing index.

Remember: ALTER TABLE is a DDL command and issues an implicit commit!

As we have seen, the primary key constraint enforces uniqueness using an index. This is the same method used by the unique constraint.

Unique

The unique constraint ensures that one or more columns defined contain unique values. If more than one column is in the constraint, then each column can have duplicate values as long as the combination of values is unique.

For example, if we place a unique constraint on the author's first and last names, then I can have multiple authors with first name John and last name Miller, but I can have only one John Miller. John Smith, Fred Miller, Steve Miller, and John Jones all will be allowed, but only one of each first, last name pair.

```
SQL> alter table author
  2    add (constraint names_un unique
(author_first_name,author_last_name));

Table altered.
```

A quick check of the indexes on the AUTHOR table will show that the constraint is being enforced using an index.

```
SQL> select
  2    index_name,
  3    table_name
  4  from user_indexes;

INDEX_NAME                          TABLE_NAME
----------------------------------  ----------------------------
NAMES_UN                            AUTHOR
AUTHOR_PK                           AUTHOR
```

We can create a unique constraint when we create the table.

```
SQL> create table editor
  2  (
  3    editor_key                  varchar2(9) not null,
  4    editor_last_name            varchar2(40),
  5    editor_first_name           varchar2(30),
  6    editor_hire_date            date,
  7    editor_active               char(1)
  8    constraint active_ck check (editor_active in ('Y','N')),
  9    constraint ed_name_un unique
(editor_first_name,editor_last_name),
 10    constraint editor_pk primary key (editor_key)
 11      using index tablespace users
 12  );

Table created.
```

As with the primary key, we can DISABLE, ENABLE and DROP the constraint.

```
SQL> alter table editor disable constraint ed_name_un;

Table altered.

SQL> alter table editor enable constraint ed_name_un;

Table altered.

SQL> alter table editor drop constraint ed_name_un;

Table altered.
```

As with the primary key, the index used to enforce the constraint is dropped whenever the constraint is disabled or dropped. When the constraint is enabled again, the index is rebuilt.

You can also create a unique constraint by creating a unique index.

```
create unique index contract_uk on
          author (author_contract_nbr);
```

The unique index performs the same function as a unique constraint; however, there is no constraint name. The index is the constraint. To remove the constraint, drop the index. There is more on indexes at the end of the chapter.

The constraints we have covered so far all impact data being inserted or updated against data already in that column. The foreign key constraint validates data against data in another column or a column in another table.

Foreign Key Constraints

A foreign key constraint will validate the values of an INSERT or UPDATE against the values in another column. Normally the column is in another table, but it could be another column in the same table. This is a parent/child relationship. The parent is the column (or columns) referenced in the foreign key. The child is the column (or columns) that contain the foreign key constraint.

When data is inserted or updated in the child column, the foreign key will verify that the value exist in the parent column. If the value does not exist, the foreign key constraint will not allow the value in the child column. Let's look at the EMP table.

```
SQL> desc emp
 Name                                    Null?     Type
 --------------------------------------- --------- ----------------
 EMP_KEY                                            VARCHAR2(9)
 JOB_KEY                                            NUMBER(5)
 PUB_KEY                                            VARCHAR2(4)
 EMP_FIRST_NAME                                     VARCHAR2(20)
 EMP_MI                                             VARCHAR2(1)
 EMP_LAST_NAME                                      VARCHAR2(30)
 EMP_DATE_OF_HIRE                                   DATE
 EMP_SALARY                                         NUMBER(6)
 MANAGER                                            VARCHAR2(9)
```

Each employee has a manager, except the manager. You can find the manager by looking at the manager column for each employee. The manager column contains the employee key of the manager for that employee. One of our business rules is that all managers must be an employee. We can enforce this rule with a foreign key constraint.

The parent column is *emp_key*. The child column is *manager*. When I insert or update a value in the *manager* column (change the employee's manager), the foreign key will first check the parent (*emp_key*) column to see that the manager exists (the *emp_key* exists in the *emp_key* column).

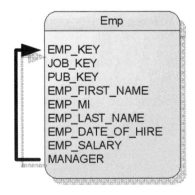

Figure 5.1: *Foreign Key on Emp Table*

First, we need to create the foreign key.

```
alter table emp
  add (constraint manger_fk foreign key (manager)
       references emp (emp_key)
       on delete set null);
```

We will discuss the ON DELETE part shortly, but first let's look at the table and how the foreign key protects our data.

```
SQL> select
  2     emp_key,
  3     emp_last_name,
  4     manager
  5   from
  6     emp;

EMP_KEY   EMP_LAST_NAME                    MANAGER
--------- -------------------------------- ---------
E101      king
E102      jackson                          E101
E103      korn                             E101
E104      linus                            E101
E105      tokheim                          E101
E106      levender                         E101
E107      johnson                          E101
E108      baker                            E101
E109      coleman                          E101
E110      brannigan                        E101
```

Here, we see that King (*emp_key* E101) is the manager for all the employees. King is getting over worked, so the boss wants us to make Baker the manager for Linus and Johnson. We can do this with an easy UPDATE.

```
SQL> update emp
  2   set manager = 'E108'
  3   where emp_key in ('E104','E107');

2 rows updated.

SQL> select
  2     emp_key,
  3     emp_last_name,
  4     manager
  5   from
  6     emp;
```

```
EMP_KEY    EMP_LAST_NAME                    MANAGER
---------  ------------------------------   ---------
E101       king
E102       jackson                          E101
E103       korn                             E101
E104       linus                            E108
E105       tokheim                          E101
E106       levender                         E101
E107       johnson                          E108
E108       baker                            E101
E109       coleman                          E101
E110       brannigan                        E101

10 rows selected.
```

No problem there. Behind that UPDATE, the foreign key made sure that E108 was listed in the *emp_key* column before it allowed the UPDATE. Now, the boss has decided that he will be King's manager. No problem, the boss's *emp_key* is E000, so we just use another UPDATE.

```
SQL> update emp
  2  set manager = 'E000'
  3  where emp_key = 'E101';
update emp
       *
ERROR at line 1:
ORA-02291: integrity constraint (PUBS.MANGER_FK) violated - parent
key not Found
```

The boss cannot be listed as King's manager, because he is not in the EMP table. More correctly, his *emp_key* is not a value in the *emp_key* column. If we add him to the table, then he can be King's manager. This example showed a foreign key on a table. The foreign key can also be used to between tables. Look at the JOB and EMP tables.

The boss just made a new rule; no one can be an employee unless they have a job (kind of obvious). In other words, when they are assigned a job, it must already be in the JOB table. The EMP table contains a job key column that matches the job key column in the JOB table. Since we want to insure that the job is defined before the employee is assigned the job, the JOB table becomes the parent table and the EMP table the child table in this foreign key relationship.

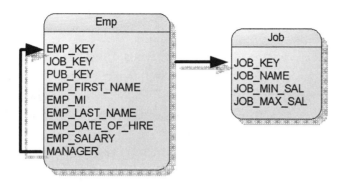

Figure 5.2: *Foreign Key Constraint Emp and Job Tables*

Let's create the constraint.

```
SQL> alter table emp
  2      add (constraint job_fk foreign key (job_key)
  3          references job (job_key)
  4          on delete cascade);

Table altered.
```

Now, when I INSERT or UPDATE the job key column in the EMP table, the foreign key constraint will check to insure that the job already exists in the JOB table (or at least the job key exist in the JOB table).

Foreign key constraints can also be disabled, enabled and dropped.

```
alter table emp disable constraint job_fk;

alter table emp enable constraint job_fk;

alter table emp drop constraint job_fk;
```

Now, let's talk about the ON DELETE part of the constraint. When we created the foreign key constraint. we included ON

DELETE SET NULL or ON DELETE CASCADE. This clause tells the database what to do with the child records when the parent record is deleted. In the example above, we created the *job_fk* constraint with ON DELETE CASCADE. This will cause the database to cascade the deletes. If I go to the JOB table and DELETE a job, all the employees that have that job will also be deleted as the DELETE will cascade to the child rows. If we use the ON DELETE SET NULL, then when we delete the parent record, the child records with that value will be set to NULL. Why would we want to cascade foreign key deletes? One great example is the STATSPACK package that Oracle provides with the database. This package has over twenty tables, and it gathers performance statistics from the database and loads them into the tables.

The statistics are gathered periodically, say once every hour. As time goes by, the STATSPACK tables will grow very large. If I only want to maintain 30 days of data, I need to delete the data that is older than 30 days. Because STATSPACK creates it tables with a foreign key ON DELETE CASCADE to one main table called *stats$snapshot*, I can delete the old rows in that one table and all the data in the other tables will also be deleted.

```
delete from stats$snapshot where snap_time < sysdate - 30;
```

This one command deletes all the data over 30 days old from all the STATSPACK tables. This is the power of ON DELETE CASCADE.

Foreign keys will allow you to make a column NULL, even if there is not a NULL in the parent table.

```
SQL> update emp
  2   set job_key = NULL
  3   where emp_key = 'E106';

1 row updated.
```

This is not surprising given that ON DELETE SET NULL will, in fact, set a column to NULL when the parent value is deleted.

When you use a foreign key on multiple columns, you can end up with invalid data in your table if you are not careful. If I have a four column foreign key, the constraint is ensuring that the combined four values are in the parent table. If one of the values in the UPDATE/INSERT contains a NULL, then none of the other values are checked. So, if I created a multi-column foreign key on the EMP table that included the *emp_key, job_key* and *pub_key* to some parent table with those columns (the PUBS schema does not have such a table so this example is hypothetical) and inserted a row with the *job_key* set to NULL, the foreign key will not check the *emp_key* or the *pub_key* values. In this way, you could enter a row with an invalid emp_key (someone who is not an employee), an invalid *pub_key* (unknown publisher), and a NULL *job_key,* and the database will accept it.

NOT NULL

The NOT NULL constraint ensures that a column does not have NULL values. Any value that is inserted or updated in that column is check to insure that it is not a NULL value. The NOT Null constraint can be named or be part of the table definition (not have a name).

```
create table editor
(
  editor_key              varchar2(9) not null,
  editor_last_name varchar2(40),
  editor_first_name varchar2(30) not null,
  editor_hire_date date,
  editor_active           char(1)
  constraint active_ck check (editor_active in ('Y','N')),
  constraint ed_name_un unique (editor_first_name,editor_last_name),
  constraint editor_pk primary key (editor_key)
    using index tablespace users
);
```

NOT NULL constraints are automatically defined on columns with primary key and unique constraints. If the table already exists, you can use the ALTER TABLE command to modify the column.

```
SQL> alter table editor modify editor_first_name not null;

Table altered.

SQL> desc editor
 Name                                      Null?    Type
 ----------------------------------------- -------- ----------------
 EDITOR_KEY                                NOT NULL VARCHAR2(9)
 EDITOR_LAST_NAME                                   VARCHAR2(40)
 EDITOR_FIRST_NAME                         NOT NULL VARCHAR2(30)
 EDITOR_HIRE_DATE                                   DATE
 EDITOR_ACTIVE                                      CHAR(1)

SQL> alter table editor modify editor_first_name null;

Table altered.

SQL> desc editor
 Name                                      Null?    Type
 ----------------------------------------- -------- ----------------
 EDITOR_KEY                                NOT NULL VARCHAR2(9)
 EDITOR_LAST_NAME                                   VARCHAR2(40)
 EDITOR_FIRST_NAME                                  VARCHAR2(30)
 EDITOR_HIRE_DATE                                   DATE
 EDITOR_ACTIVE                                      CHAR(1)
```

Executing the second example does not change the values in the column; it allows the column to accept NULLs. By default, columns will accept NULLs.

The final constraint is used to insure that values inserted/updated meet a specific condition. It is called a check constraint.

Check Constraint

The job of the check constraint is to insure that updated or inserted values meet a specific condition. Like the WHERE clause, the check condition must return a TRUE or FALSE. TRUE and the value is accepted by the constraint, FALSE and the value is rejected. In the EDITOR table, we included a check constraint on the *editor_active* column that insures that the value is either Y or N.

```
create table editor
(
  editor_key              varchar2(9) not null,
  editor_last_name  varchar2(40),
  editor_first_name varchar2(30) not null,
  editor_hire_date  date,
  editor_active           char(1)
  constraint active_ck check (editor_active in ('Y','N')),
  constraint ed_name_un unique (editor_first_name,editor_last_name),
  constraint editor_pk primary key (editor_key)
    using index tablespace users
);
```

Check constraints are limited. You cannot use subqueries within your check constraints. A check constraint can reference another column, but it can only reference the value of the row being checked. You cannot reference sysdate, currval, nextval, level, rowid, uid, user or userenv.

```
SQL> alter table editor
  2    add (constraint hire_ck check (editor_hire_date > (SYSDATE -
30)));
  add (constraint hire_ck check (editor_hire_date > (SYSDATE -30)))
                                                               *
ERROR at line 2:
ORA-02436: date or system variable wrongly specified in CHECK
constraint
```

You cannot reference another table's columns. You can have more that one check constraint on a column, and the values being checked must pass all check constraint on that column before being acceptable. A check constraint can also check multiple columns.

So, a check constraint is limited in its ability to validate data. If you need a more capable check, you must implement it as a trigger. Triggers are beyond the scope of this book but are covered in Easy Oracle PL/SQL and in the many PL/SQL books available.

I'm here to enforce your constraint!

Deferred Constraints

Normally, constraints are checked as data is inserted or updated in the row. When a row is inserted, all the constraints are checked and the row either accepted or rejected. You can, however, defer the constraint checking until the transaction commits. In that case, the row is inserted into the table and constraints are not checked until the COMMIT is issued. If the row then fails, it is removed from the table. You can change the status of the constraints by setting them as DEFERRED or IMMEDIATE. In order to change the constraint, it must be deferrable.

```
SQL> set constraint active_ck deferred;
set constraint active_ck deferred
*
ERROR at line 1:
ORA-02447: cannot defer a constraint that is not deferrable
```

Here, the *active_ck* constraint was not created as deferrable. In fact, none of the constraints we have created so far can be DEFFERED. Let's recreate the *job_fk* as a deferrable constraint.

```
SQL> alter table emp drop constraint job_fk;

Table altered.
```

Easy Oracle SQL

```
SQL>  alter table emp
  2       add (constraint job_fk foreign key (job_key)
  3            references job (job_key)
  4            on delete cascade deferrable);

Table altered.

SQL> set constraint job_fk deferred;

Constraint set.

SQL> set constraint job_fk immediate;

Constraint set.
```

First, I drop the current constraint and recreate it with the deferrable key work. Now, I can defer the constraint and reset it back to IMMEDIATE. This seems a bit complicated, so why would you want to defer a constraint? One example is with foreign key constraints. You can, and should, set up foreign key constraints to insure that the data in your tables is correctly related. Once the foreign keys are in place, you must insure that data is inserted/updated to the parent first, then to the child tables.

With a number of foreign key constraints in place, you could run into the situation where you cannot get the data into the tables without violating at least one foreign key. If I could just get the data loaded, then the check the foreign keys the data would be accepted. Here is where the deferred constraint is useful. By deferring the foreign key constraints, you can get the data into the tables and then validate it against the foreign keys. Invalid data is still rejected.

You can never have too many foreign keys!

Protection vs. Validation

Through out this section, I have talked about constraints protecting your data. The job of the constraint is to insure that the data you INSERT/UPDATE meets the requirements set forth in the constraints, to protect your data. Many users use constraints to validate their data. Basically, here is a row, throw it at the database and see if it accepts it.

While this approach works, it has a significant impact on the database performance. The Oracle database assumes that the data will be accepted. The database logs the changes in the undo/redo logs, updates the table (and any indexes) before checking the constraints. If the data fails, all those changes must be undone.

Why does the database implement constraint checking in this way? Because, it is the most efficient way for the database to store and protect your data. Your application is responsible for validating the data. The database catches those pieces of data that the program let slip through, thus providing integrity protection.

Now that we can insure the quality of our data by implementing
constraints, we need to look at some of the database objects that
allow us to better access that data. We start by covering views
and materialized views.

Views and Materialized Views

There are two kinds of views in an Oracle database, and they are
very different in their implementation and use. One is stored as
pure SQL, while the other creates a table that it maintains. We
will start with the simple view.

Views

A view is a named SQL statement that is stored in the database.
You use a view in much the same way you use a database table.
When you query from a view, the database takes the stored SQL
statement and creates a table in memory. Because it is defined as
a SQL statement, a view can join tables or limit the number of
rows. There are two primary uses of views:

- Reduce the complexity of a SQL statement

- Restrict access to data.

We can reduce the complexity of our queries by creating a view
instead of using subqueries. In the last chapter, we created a
query that lists the names of stores with above average sales.

```
select
  initcap (store_name) "Store Name"
from
 (select
    store_name,
    avg(quantity) qty
  from
    store join sales using (store_key)
```

```
   group by store_name) a
where qty > (select
                avg(qty) Average_Sales
             from (select
                      store_name,
                      avg(quantity) qty
                   from
                     store join sales using (store_key)
                   group by store_name))
order by qty;
```

The query above contains a nested subquery used twice. I can replace the subquery with a view to reduce the complexity.

```
SQL> create view avg_store as
  2    select
  3      store_name,
  4      avg(quantity) qty
  5    from
  6      store join sales using (store_key)
  7    group by store_name;

View created.
```

Our query is simplified by using the view instead of the subquery.

```
SQL> select
  2      initcap (store_name) "Store Name"
  3    from
  4      avg_store
  5    where qty > (select
  6                    avg(qty) Average_Sales
  7                 from avg_store)
  8    order by qty;

Store Name
--------------------------------------
Wee Bee Books
Books For Dummies
Eaton Books
Hot Wet And Mushy Books
Borders
```

The view *avg_store* is used just like a table. Visually, the database creates the view in memory and then selects from it. In reality, the view SQL is combined with your query, and the resulting query is executed. The complexity is reduced only for the user.

The other use of a view is to limit a user's access to some of the data. If the stores needed access to the PUBS database, we might want to limit their ability to see other stores' sales data. We could create a view of the SALES table for each store and grant them access to the view, not the actual SALES table. For example, my favorite bookstore, Ignoramus and Dufus, has a store key of S110. We can create a view of the SALES table for Ignoramus and Dufus that contains sales data only for their store.

```
SQL> create view sales_s110 as
  2  select *
  3  from sales
  4  where store_key = 'S110';

View created.

SQL> select * from sales_s110;

STOR BOOK_K ORDER_NUMBER         ORDER_DAT QUANTITY
---- ------ -------------------- --------- ----------
S110 B102   O110                 04-JAN-04        160
S110 B103   O111                 04-JAN-04        100
S110 B104   O112                 05-JAN-04        100
S110 B105   O113                 05-JAN-04        150
S110 B105   O165                 29-MAR-04        700
S110 B106   O166                 02-APR-04        100
S110 B102   O167                 02-APR-04       1900
S110 B101   O168                 02-APR-04        300
S110 B103   O169                 03-APR-04        100

9 rows selected.
```

Now, Ignoramus and Dufus can query all they want, and they will only see their data.

I can only see me in this view!

The example above is a simple view, while the first example is a complex view. A simple view queries only one table, does not group rows or use functions. A simple view can be inserted/updated/deleted because it directly relates to the table it is created on. A complex view is, of course, any view that is not a simple view.

A simple view is updatable.

```
SQL> update sales_s110
  2   set quantity = 800
  3   where order_number = 'O165';

1 row updated.

SQL> select * from sales_s110;

STOR BOOK_K ORDER_NUMBER          ORDER_DAT  QUANTITY
---- ------ --------------------- ---------- ----------
S110 B102   O110                  04-JAN-04       160
S110 B103   O111                  04-JAN-04       100
S110 B104   O112                  05-JAN-04       100
S110 B105   O113                  05-JAN-04       150
S110 B105   O165                  29-MAR-04       800
S110 B106   O166                  02-APR-04       100
S110 B102   O167                  02-APR-04      1900
S110 B101   O168                  02-APR-04       300
S110 B103   O169                  03-APR-04       100
```

If you do not want the view to be updatable, create it with the read only option.

```
SQL> create view sales_s109 as
  2  select *
  3  from sales
  4  where store_key = 'S109'
  5  with read only;

View created.
```

The view *sales_s109* is read only.

If you need to recreate a view, you can use the CREATE or REPLACE command, and all grants will be preserved.

```
SQL> create or replace view sales_s109 as
  2  select *
  3  from sales
  4  where store_key in ('S109','S108')
  5  with read only;

View created.
```

Notice that with the CREATE or REPLACE command, we do not have to first drop the view.

We can also rename the columns in our view.

```
SQL> create or replace view sales_s109
  2     (key_book, key_store, numb_order, date_num, qty)
  3  as
  4  select *
  5  from sales
  6  where store_key in ('S109','S108')
  7  with read only;

View created.

SQL> select * from sales_s109;

KEY_ KEY_ST NUMB_ORDER            DATE_NUM        QTY
---- ------ -------------------- --------- ----------
S108 B103   O108                 04-JAN-04       100
S109 B102   O109                 04-JAN-04      1020
S109 B106   O114                 05-JAN-04       100
S108 B107   O115                 07-JAN-04       100
```

Complex views contain table joins, functions or groups. Complex views do not map back to the underlying tables. If we group our sales by store, each row in my view is an aggregate of the rows in the underlying tables.

```
create view avg_store as
select
  store_name,
  avg(quantity) qty
from
  store join sales using (store_key)
group by store_name;
```

The example above contains a GROUP BY clause and a multi-row function. This view is not updatable. A view is not updatable if:

- Contains a multi row function

- Contains a *group by* clause

- Contains the *distinct* key word.

- Uses the *rownum* key word.

If the view joins more than one table and does not violate the rules defined above, you can update one table's data at a time. What happens if you have a simple view and add a row that the view will not display?

Here is our *sales_s110* view definition.

```
create view sales_s110 as
select *
from sales
where store_key = 'S110';

SQL> insert into sales_s110
  2  values ('B104','S106','O200',SYSDATE,300);

1 row created.

SQL> select * from sales_s110
  2  ;
```

```
STOR  BOOK_K  ORDER_NUMBER           ORDER_DAT   QUANTITY
----  ------  --------------------   ---------   ----------
S110  B102    O110                   04-JAN-04        160
S110  B103    O111                   04-JAN-04        100
S110  B104    O112                   05-JAN-04        100
S110  B105    O113                   05-JAN-04        150
S110  B105    O165                   29-MAR-04        800
S110  B106    O166                   02-APR-04        100
S110  B102    O167                   02-APR-04       1900
S110  B101    O168                   02-APR-04        300
S110  B103    O169                   03-APR-04        100

9 rows selected.
```

Our view will only show us rows with a store key of S110. But, it will allow you to insert a row with another store key. To insure that this is not possible, you can create the view with the CHECK option, and all INSERT/UPDATE operations will be validated against the WHERE clause in the view.

```
SQL> create or replace view sales_s110 as
  2  select *
  3  from sales
  4  where store_key = 'S110'
  5  with check option constraint s110_view_ck;

View created.

SQL> insert into sales_s110
  2  values ('B104','S106','O200',SYSDATE,300);
insert into sales_s110
             *
ERROR at line 1:
ORA-01402: view WITH CHECK OPTION where-clause violation
```

The CHECK option creates a constraint on the view.

If we no longer need the view, we can delete it from the database by dropping it.

```
SQL> drop view sales_s110;

View dropped.
```

While views are stored in the database as a SQL statement and are created as needed, a materialized view is created as a table, and physically stored in the database.

Materialized Views

Materialized views (Mview) are very much like a regular Oracle table, except that they are based on one or more tables. They can be simple or complex, read only, or updatable. Because an Mview is a physical table, changes are managed by updating the effected rows in the Mview when the underlying tables change. Updating an Mview is called refreshing it. There are two types of refresh: fast and full.

In a full refresh, the Mview is truncated and rebuild from the underlying tables. In a fast refresh, only the changes are updated in the Mview. A forced refresh tells the Mview to try and execute a fast refresh, and if that fails, execute a full refresh. In order to execute a fast refresh, the underlying tables must have a materialized view log. This log records changes to the table so that the Mview can retrieve them.

Mviews are normally used to aggregate information in a data warehouse database. They can also be used in replicating data from one database to another. Unlike normal views, INSERTs/UPDATEs/DELETESs of Mview require implementing advanced replication, which is far beyond the scope of this book. The Mview can be writable, which allows the data to be modified; however, the changes are not propagated back to the underlying tables and are lost when the Mview refreshes.

We are going to create an Mview similar to the normal view we already created. The query we will use is below.

```
select
  store_name,
  avg(quantity) qty
from
  store join sales using (store_key)
group by store_name;
```

Now, we create the materialized view.

```
SQL> create materialized view avg_sales2
  2   refresh complete
  3   NEXT sysdate + 5/(24*60)
  4   as
  5   select
  6     store_name,
  7     avg(quantity) qty
  8   from
  9     store join sales using (store_key)
 10   group by store_name;
Materialized view created.
```

Because our Mview is complex (group by), we have to execute a complete refresh. Notice that the NEXT clause tells the Mview to refresh every five minutes. We can make a simple materialized view that allows fast refresh.

We want to be able to execute a fast refresh, so we need Mview logs on the underlying table, SALES.

```
SQL> create materialized view log on sales;
Materialized view log created.
```

Now, let's make create an Mview that will limit access to data in the SALES table.

```
SQL> create materialized view sales_s110_v2
  2   refresh fast
  3   next sysdate + 1/(24*60)
  4   as
  5   select * from sales
  6   where store_key = 'S110';
Materialized view created.
```

The above Mview will refresh fast using the Mview log on the SALES table and will refresh every minute. It will never be more than a minute behind the underlying table. Alternately, you can refresh on COMMIT. When changes are committed to the underlying tables, the Mview will execute a fast refresh.

Another advantage of using a materialized view is the ability to have the optimizer rewrite appropriate queries to use the materialized view instead of the underlying table. The query optimizer can use materialized views by automatically recognizing when an existing materialized view can and should be used to satisfy a request. It then transparently rewrites the request to use the materialized view. Queries are then directed to the materialized view and not to the underlying tables, which should result in a significant performance gain. To take advantage of this capability, a DBA must grant the user some rights. Since we made PUBS a DBA, the user PUBS already has these rights.

```
SQL> grant query rewrite to pubs;
SQL> grant create materialized view to pubs;
SQL> alter session set query_rewrite_enabled = true;
```

You also need some of the parameters set in the database initialization file or the *initSID.ora*. You will need help from your DBA for this. The database must be using the cost based optimizer, and the following parameters must be set.

```
query_rewrite_enabled = true
query_rewrite_integrity = enforced
```

Now, I need to recreate my Mview enabling query rewrite.

```
SQL> create materialized view agg_sales
  2    enable query rewrite
  3    as
  4    select
  5      store_key,
  6      avg(quantity) qty
  7    from
  8      sales
  9    group by store_key;

Materialized view create
```

Notice that I added the clause to ENABLE the query rewrite function on this Mview. Now, I am going to turn on AUTOTRACE and run a simple query to show that the database rewrote the query.

```
SQL> set autotrace on explain
SQL> select
  2     store_key,
  3     avg(quantity)
  4  from
  5     sales
  6  group by store_key;

STOR AVG(QUANTITY)
---- -------------
B104           300
S101           545
...
S123           100
S124           100

15 rows selected.


Execution Plan
-----------------------------------------------------------
   0      SELECT STATEMENT Optimizer=ALL_ROWS (Cost=3 Card=15
Bytes=25
          5)

   1    0   MAT_VIEW REWRITE ACCESS (FULL) OF 'AGG_SALES' (MAT_VIEW
RE
          WRITE) (Cost=3 Card=15 Bytes=255)
```

Notice that my query uses the SALES table but the execution plan shows that the database knew that it had already calculated the averages, so it rewrote the query to use the *agg_sales* Mview. This saved the database from recalculating the data stored in the Mview. This example is trivial, but think about the benefit in a data warehouse with thousands of stores and many millions of orders. Here, the benefit would be profound.

This is a brief introduction to materialized views. They are actually very complex and powerful database objects. In a data warehouse, Mview are very complex and normally only refreshed when new data has been loaded. When used in replication, most Mview are simple and refresh often every minute.

The Mview is an actual table in the database and changes to underlying tables are updated by refreshing the data in the Mview. Normal views are stored as SQL and are combined with the query that calls them. A normal view is used to reduce complexity or limit access to data.

Sequences

A sequence is a database object that provides a number when requested. Like a view, a sequence is just the definition and the current number. When a sequence is asks for a number, it looks at the current number and provides the next number as per the sequence definition.

```
SQL> create sequence pubs1;

Sequence created.

SQL> select pubs1.nextval from dual;

   NEXTVAL
----------
         1

SQL> select pubs1.nextval from dual;

   NEXTVAL
----------
         2
```

In the example above, we created a sequence called *pubs1*. We use the NEXTVAL function to retrieve the next value. You can get the current value by calling the CURRVAL function. You must call the NEXTVAL function before calling the CURRVAL function, or you will get an error. There is no current value to the sequence until the next value has been called at least once.

When you create the sequence, you have a lot of flexibility as to how the sequence generates the next number.

```
SQL> create sequence pubs2
  2   start with 8
  3   increment by 2
  4   maxvalue 10000
  5   cycle
  6   cache 5;

Sequence created.

SQL> select pubs2.nextval from dual;

   NEXTVAL
----------
         8
```

The sequence *pubs2* will start at number eight and increment by twos to 10000 and then start over. Let's cover each of their parameters:

- START WITH – defines the first number of the sequence. Default is one.

- INCREMENT – defines how many to add to get the next values. Default is one.

- MINVALUE – defines the lowest value of the sequence when the sequence is created to count down (increment by a minus number).

- MAXVALUE – defines the largest value of the sequence. Default is 10E23.

- CYCLE/NOCYCLE – tells the sequence to start over once it reaches the maxvalue or minvalue. The default is NOCYCLE.

- CACHE/NOCACHE – tells the database how many numbers to cache in memory. The default is 20. So, if the sequence is starting at one, the database will cache 1..20 and set the sequence at 21. The database will answer the NEXTVAL request from the numbers in memory. Once those numbers are used, the database will load 20 more numbers in memory. If the database is shutdown, all sequence numbers in memory will be lost. When the database restarts, it will look at the number for the sequence and load the next 20 into memory, setting the sequence forward by 20. This improves response but will lose some numbers. Setting the NOCACHE will cause the database not to cache any numbers in memory.

Sequences are relatively simple objects designed to provide a series of numbers. No call to NEXTVAL will result in the same number unless the sequence cycles. One of the main uses of a sequence is to provide a primary key for a table where the rows do not naturally define a unique number. In our AUTHOR table, the primary key is author_key, and it is formatted as A101, A102, etc. I can use a sequence to generate this key.

```
SQL> select pubs2.nextval from dual;

   NEXTVAL
----------
        12

SQL> insert into author values
  2  (
  3      'A'||to_char (pubs2.nextval + 100),
  4      'thumbmasher',
  5      'philbert',
  6     '457-934-2642',
  7     '1320 leaning tree ln',
  8     'pie town',
  9     'IL',
 10     '57307',
 11     '7896');

1 row created.

SQL> select author_key, author_last_name from author;
```

```
AUTHOR_KEY   AUTHOR_LAST_NAME
-----------  ----------------------------------------
A101         jones
A102         hester
A103         weaton
A104         jeckle
A105         withers
A106         petty
A107         clark
A108         mee
A109         shagger
A110         smith
A114         thumbmasher

11 rows selected.
```

Remember that we created *pubs2* to increment by two. Once you learn PL/SQL, you will be able to create a trigger that will automatically create the key on INSERT.

From the simple sequence, we move to one of the most complicated object in the database, the index.

Indexes

So, you go to the library to find a book to read. It is summer, and you have time on your hands and are not sure what you want. You probably browse the shelves looking for something that might interest you. When you're not sure what you want, this is a pretty easy access method, browsing the shelves. But a database never browses for a row. It is always looking for a particular row or rows.

So, let's go back to the library and look for a particular book. In this instance, you would not go and browse the shelves; you would head for the card catalog. It could take you hours to find a book by searching the shelves, while it will take only minutes to look up the book and go directly to the shelf where the book is located. This is because all of the books in the library are numbered using the Dewey Decimal system. Sometimes, you are not sure which book you want but know the general subject.

You can look up the subject in the card catalog and then go to the shelves and look at a range of books.

Oracle uses basically the same system, except that the card catalog is an index and the book number becomes the rowid. When a query asks for a specific row of data, an index allows the database to look up the rowid of that specific row and directly retrieve it. Otherwise, the database must start at the beginning of the table and check each row to find the data it wants.

```
select *
from author
where author_key = 'A104';
```

In the example above, I am looking for a row in the AUTHOR table where the *author_key* is A104. If I have an index on the author key, the database will use that index to quickly find the correct row.

```
AUTHOR_KEY  AUTHOR_LAST_NAME                            AUTHOR_FIRST_NAME
----------- ------------------------------------------- --------------------
AUTHOR_PHONE AUTHOR_STREET                              AUTHOR_CITY         AU
----------- ------------------------------------------- -------------------- --
AUTHO AUTHOR_CONTRACT_NBR
----- -------------------
A104        jeckle                                      pierre
543-333-9241 3671 old fort st                            north hollywood    CA
91607               6602
```

```
Execution Plan
----------------------------------------------------------
   0      SELECT STATEMENT Optimizer=ALL_ROWS (Cost=1 Card=1 Bytes=73)
   1    0   TABLE ACCESS (BY INDEX ROWID) OF 'AUTHOR' (TABLE) (Cost=1
            Card=1 Bytes=73)

   2    1     INDEX (UNIQUE SCAN) OF 'AUTHOR_PK' (INDEX (UNIQUE)) (Cos
              t=0 Card=1)
```

In the example above, I pulled the execution plan from the database. Notice that the database used the *author_pk* index (which is on the author key) to find the *rowed,* and then performed a table access by *rowid* to retrieve the row (read from inside to outside). It basically looked up the book title (*author_key*) in the card catalog (index) and went directly to the shelve (table) and retrieved the book (row).

An index is like a librarian with attitude!

So, an index is a pairing of a column (or columns) value and the *rowid* for that row. In our example with the PUBS database, there is not much difference between using an index and scanning the entire table. That is because we only have ten or so rows of data in our table. If we had hundreds of thousands of rows, the index would show a significant speed improvement over scanning the entire table. If there were only ten books in the library, you would also skip the card catalog. An index can also provide a range if values for the database to retrieve from the table. Let's look at an index and how the database creates it.

```
SQL> create index sales_book
  2  on sales (book_key);

Index created.
```

In the example above, we created an index called *sales_book* on the book key of the SALES table. We chose this index because many of our queries use the *book_key* in the WHERE clause filters. Since the query is filtering by book key, it can use the index and collect the rowids of rows that pass the filters.

Database Objects

Indexes also speed UPDATEs and DELETEs. Remember, to DELETE or UPDATE a row, the database must first find the row. The index helps the database quickly find the row.

B-Tree Index

By default, the Oracle creates a b_tree index. In a b-tree, you walk the branches until you get to the node that has the data you want to use. In the classic b-tree structure, there are branches from the top that lead to leaf nodes that contain the data. If I wanted to find the rowid for the number 28 in the b-tree defined in Figure 5.3, I would start at the top or header block.

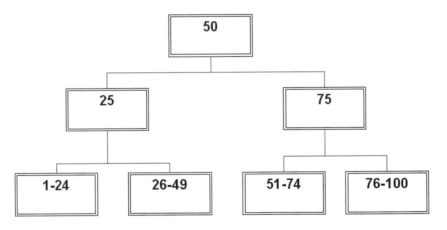

Figure 5.3: *Classic B-Tree Structure*

Is my number greater or less that 50? Well 28 is less than 50, so I move to the branch marked 25. Is 28 greater or less that 25? Since 28 is greater than 25, I move to the leaf node marked 26-49. I scan this node for the rowid of the number 28. The key to the b-tree in Figure 5.3 is that I can find any number from one to 100 by reading no more than three nodes.

The Oracle database implements the b-tree index in a little different manner. An Oracle b-tree starts with only two nodes, one header and one leaf. The header contains a pointer to the life block and the values stored in the leaf block. As the index grows leaf bocks are added to the index (Figure 5.4).

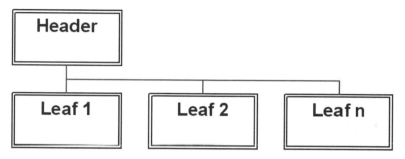

Figure 5.4: *Oracle B-tree Index*

To find a specific row, we look at the header to find the range of values in each leaf and then go directly to the leaf node that contains the value we are looking for. In the index in Figure 5.4, any row can be found by reading two nodes. Since the header contains only pointers to leaf blocks, a single header node can support a very large number (hundreds) of leaf nodes.

If the header block fills, then a new header block is established, and the former header node becomes a branch node. This is called a three level b-tree (Figure 5.5).

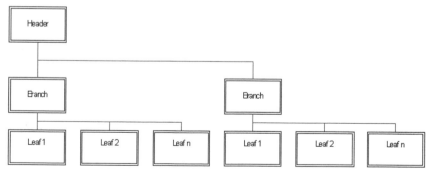

Figure 5.5: *Tree Level B-tree*

In Figure 5.5, you can find any value in any leaf node by reading no more than three blocks. I can also create a multicolumn index, also called a concatenated or complex index.

```
SQL> create index sales_keys
  2  on sales (book_key, store_key, order_number);

Index created.
```

Here, we created an index called *sales_keys* on three columns of the SALES table. A multicolumn index can be used by the database but only from the first or lead column. Our *sales_keys* index can be used in the following query.

```
select
  order_number,
  quantity
from
  sales
where
  book_key = 'B103';
```

Note that the lead column of the index is the *book_key*, so the database can use the index in the query above. I can also use the *sales_keys* index in the queries below.

```
select
  order_number,
  quantity
from
  sales
where
  book_key = 'B103'
and
  store_key = 'S105'
and
  order_number = 'O168';
```

However, the database cannot use that index in the following query because the WHERE clause does not contain the index lead column.

```
select
  order_number,
  quantity
from
  sales
where
  store_key = 'S105'
and
  order_number = 'O168';
```

Also, note that in the query below, the database can answer the query from the index and so will not access the table at all.

```
select
  order_number
from
  sales
where
  store_key = 'S105'
and
  book_key = 'B108';
```

As you can see, b-tree indexes are very powerful. You must remember that a multicolumn index cannot skip over columns, so the lead index column must be in the WHERE clause filters. Oracle has used b-tree indexes for many years, and they are appropriate from most of your indexing needs. However, the Oracle database provides specialized indexes that can provide additional capabilities; the bit-mapped index and the function-based index.

Bitmapped Index

The bit mapped index uses a bitmap instead of a b-tree to represent the data/rowid pairs. A bit mapped index is very fast at locating data; however, it is very slow at updating or inserting index values. For this reason, bitmapped indexes are used mostly on static data such as in a data warehouse. A bitmapped index functions best on low cardinality columns, columns with a small number of distinct values. The bitmap created for the index is as wide as the cardinality and as long and the number of rows.

If our publishing company divided its operations into regions, East, West, North, and South, the *regions* column would have four distinct values or a cardinality of four. If the table contained 100 rows, then a bitmap on region would be four wide and 100 long. But since we are talking about computer bits that are very small, this index would be very small also. Remember, a kilobyte is a 1028 bytes or 8224 bits.

Let's look at what the bitmapped index would look like. Each value is a TRUE or FALSE. So, if the bit map was set up as E, W, N, S, then an East value would be 1,0,0,0. A North value would be 0,0,1,0. Notice that the correct value is a one and the incorrect values are zeroes. With the corresponding *rowid,* our bit map would look like Table 5.1 below.

Rowid	E	W	N	S
00100	1	0	0	0
00056	0	0	1	0
00206	0	0	0	1
10045	0	1	0	0

Table 5.1: *Example of a Bitmapped Index*

The rowids I used are just examples. rowids are actually large alphanumeric numbers. This example looks simple enough. If I had 1000 rows, then my bitmap would be five columns wide and 1000 rows long. What makes bitmaps so fast is that comparing ones and zeroes is what microprocessors do best. In fact, they can compare multiple values at the same time, some as many as 64 values at a time. To search the bitmap, the database uses the WHERE clause filters to create a mask. In the query below, I want all rows from region West.

```
select
  office_num,
  sales
from
  year_2005_sales
where
  region = 'WEST';
```

Since I am looking for West, the database creates the mask 1,0,0,0. Now, I can use the mask and run down the bitmap using the AND/OR function to compare the mask with the row values. Those that return TRUE, we grab the rowids (00100) and access the table, retrieving the rows. One of the unique abilities of the bitmapped index is that multiple indexes can be used by one query. It is the only type of index that the Oracle database will use more that one index to access a table in a single query. The reason is that the bitmapped indexes can be combined, and one mask used to scan multiple indexes at the same time.

```
select
  office_num,
  sales
from
  all_year_sales
where
  region = "WEST"
and
  year   = 2005;
```

Here, we have two columns to filter by, and both have a bitmapped index. Since the bitmaps have the same number of rows, they can be compared directly. In the first example, comparing the value mask to the index resulted in a one or zero (TRUE or FALSE). I can compare multiple indexes, place the results side by side, and compare them to produce a final result.

Lastly, bitmapped indexes can be created on the join of two tables. Queries that join the same tables can use the index to filter both tables at the join.

Database Objects

```
create bitmap index store_sales on
  sales (store_key)
from
  sales join store using (store_key);
```

This creates a bitmap of the table join. It is the same as building an index on the store_key of the two tables and then joining them.

So, bitmap indexes have two real advantages; they are very fast, and more than one can be used to satisfy a query. But, they also have problems, INSERTs/UPDATEs take a performance hit when bitmap indexes are used, and they need to be used on low cardinality columns. So, bitmapped indexes are most useful with static data or data warehouses.

Function Based Indexes (FBI)

In the examples above, we have used filters on columns to limit the rows returned. The indexes used those filters to locate the needed rows before accessing the table. A problem arises when we filter on a column in a function.

```
select
  author_last_name
  author_contract_nbr
from
  author
where upper(author_last_name) = 'PETTY';
```

Even if you have an index on the *author_last_name* column, the database can not use it because you are filtering on *upper(author_last_name)*.

Why will you not use my index?

To use an index, you need to create a function based index (FBI). A FBI is simply an index that uses the function so that the database can make direct comparisons between the index values and the filter values.

```
create index auth_last_nm_fbi on
  author (upper(author_last_name));
```

The FBI, *auth_last_nm_fbi,* can be used in any query to filter the rows on *upper(author_last_name).* The key to using FBIs is that the functions in the WHERE clause must exactly match the function in the FBI. Like materialized views, FBIs also require that you use the cost based optimizer and enable QUERY REWRITE. Talk to your DBA concerning these parameters.

Creating Indexes

The same format is used no matter which type of index you are creating.

```
Create unique|bitmap index <index name> on
<table name> (col1, col2, col3,…);
```

A unique index was covered in the discussion of constraints as well as uses to both speed queries and enforce that each value in the column is unique.

```
create unique index auth_contract on
  author(author_contract_nbr);

create bitmap index bk_auth on
  book_author(book_key, author_key);

create index half_sales on
  sales (quantity/2);
```

If you do not define the type of index, the database creates a non-unique b-tree index.

If you decide that you want to change an index, from unique to non-unique for example, you have to drop the current index and recreate it in the new type. You can rebuild indexes using the ALTER INDEX command. When you rebuild an index, the database uses the current index if it is valid to create the new index. Once the new index is created, the old index is dropped.

If you specify online, the database will continue to use the old index until the new one is completed and then switches to the new index. You can also use the rebuild to move the index to another tablespace.

```
alter index bk_auth rebuild online;

alter index bk_auth rebuild tablespace indx_ts;
```

If the current index is not valid, then the database rebuilds the index from the original table. Invalid indexes are not used. An index becomes invalid when the *rowids* in the index no longer match the *rowids* in the table. If I rebuild a table, all the indexes created on that table will be marked invalid and must be rebuilt.

As a last point on indexes, you must be careful in indexing your database. Each index adds overhead, having to be updated with every change to that column in the table. If your database uses static data and only select queries, then over indexing will not hurt performance. But, most databases have a mix of INSERTs, UPDATEs, DELETEs and SELECTs. Too many indexes can have a significant negative impact on INSERTs, UPDATEs, and DELETEs.

There are many other objects in the Oracle database, but we are focusing on those that impact SQL. Most of the other objects belong in the realm of the DBA and are beyond the scope of this book.

Indexing Foreign Keys

We talked about foreign keys and how they enforced a parent child relationship. One problem with foreign keys is that when you UPDATE/INSERT to the child column, you must scan the parent column to validate the key. If the parent is not a primary key, this can result in constantly reading the entire table to validate the child value. Placing an index on the parent column will allow the foreign key to validate the child with the index, avoiding the costly full table scan.

When you start designing your database, you need to develop a naming scheme. This will allow you to determine the function of objects in the database. Tables are pretty easy, but indexes are normally left out. You should name each object so that you know what it does. The *emp_job_fdx* index could be the index on the *emp_job_fk* constraint. A primary key index could be *name_pk*, a unique index *name_udx*.

Sometimes, you can find that the database over indexes, causing performance problems on INSERTs and UPDATEs. You must

---

determine which indexes you can remove to improve performance. If you unknowingly delete an index on a foreign key, the performance impact may be drastic. By using a logical naming convention, you will know by the object name why you placed it into the database in the first place.

Conclusion

This chapter focused on those parts of the database that protect our data and enhance our ability to retrieve and manipulate it. We started with protecting our data using constraints, then moved to objects that make the database more efficient and effective.

Constraints insure that bad data is not allowed in the database. They either validate the data on INSERT/UPDATE or on COMMIT. Primary keys define a unique identifier for each row of a table, and in a properly normalized database, each table will have a primary key. Foreign keys define a parent-child relationship. Any changes in the child must already be in the parent or the operation fails. Like a primary key, a unique constraint insures that each value, or combination of values in a multicolumn constraint, is unique. A check constraint validates the values against the check values and allows or rejects the change. All of these constraints are used to protect your data. Your application is still responsible for validating the data.

Views are SQL stored in the database and used as a table. They can be used to simplify queries. The database combines the query and the view to execute the query and return the required rows.

A materialized view is a physical table created from a query. It is used to pre-aggregate or pre-join tables. Simple materialized views can fast refresh, applying only changed data from the base tables. Complex materialized views must execute a full refresh, which involves truncating the view and recreating it from the base tables. The database can also rewrite queries on the fly to use the pre-aggregated data in a materialized view.

Indexes are used to speed access in SELECTs, UPDATEs and DELETEs. They allow the database to lookup the *rowid* of the requested rows and retrieve them directly from the table. Without an index, the database must scan the entire table from front to back to find the requested rows. If a table is rebuilt, then all indexes on that table will be invalid and must also be rebuilt. Bitmapped indexes are used with static data or data warehouses. They are extremely efficient but pay a heavy penalty when they are updated as data changes.

Function based indexes (FBI) allow an index to be built using a function on the column. The function in the FBI must exactly match the function in the query to be used. You must also use the cost based optimizer when using FBIs. Finally, every index added to a database will impact INSERTs, UPDATEs and DELETEs on the underlying tables. You must always trade off the increase in speed against the penalty of maintaining the index.

From here, you have the skills to start interacting with your Oracle database. I hope you followed along with the examples after loading the PUBS database. SQL is like any other language, be it Spanish, Java or C++. You have to use it to keep your skills up. Feel free to use the PUBS database to practice your SQL.

Further Reading

This book has been an introduction to SQL using the Oracle database. Most of the examples will run on any relational database that implements ANSI SQL. Some databases don't implement all the features discussed. For example, many small database systems do not support subqueries.

Your next step in this process is to become proficient in PL/SQL, a structured language built into the Oracle database. For this I recommend:

Easy Oracle PL/SQL by John Garmany from Rampant TechPress

For further information on how Oracle executes SQL within the database I recommend:

Oracle SQL Tuning & CBO Internals by Kimberly Floss from Rampant TechPress.

For advanced SQL tuning:

Oracle High-Performance SQL Tuning by Don Burleson from Oracle Press.

Index

About John Garmany

Colonel John Garmany is a graduate of West Point, an Airborne Ranger and a retired Lt. Colonel with 20+ years of IT experience.

John is an OCP Certified Oracle DBA with a Master's Degree in Information Systems, a Graduate Certificate in Software Engineering, and a BS degree (Electrical Engineering) from West Point.

A respected Oracle expert and author, John serves as a writer for Oracle Internals, DBAZine and Builder.com. John is the author of "Logical Database Design - Principles & Practices" by CRC Press, the "Oracle9iAS Administration Handbook" by Oracle Press and "Oracle Replication - Snapshot, Multi-master & Materialized Views Scripts" and "Oracle SQL*Plus Reports - Fast reporting with SQL and SQL*Plus" by Rampant TechPress.

About Mike Reed

When he first started drawing, Mike Reed drew just to amuse himself. It wasn't long, though, before he knew he wanted to be an artist. Today he does illustrations for children's books, magazines, catalogs, and ads.

He also teaches illustration at the College of Visual Art in St. Paul, Minnesota. Mike Reed says, "Making pictures is like acting — you can paint yourself into the action." He often paints on the computer, but he also draws in pen and ink and paints in acrylics. He feels that learning to draw well is the key to being a successful artist.

Mike is regarded as one of the nation's premier illustrators and is the creator of the popular "Flame Warriors" illustrations at www.flamewarriors.com, a website devoted to Internet insults. "To enter his Flame Warriors site is sort of like entering a hellish Sesame Street populated by Oscar the Grouch and 83 of his relatives." – Los Angeles Times. (http://redwing.hutman.net/%7Emreed/warriorshtm/lat.htm)

Mike Reed has always enjoyed reading. As a young child, he liked the Dr. Seuss books. Later, he started reading biographies and war stories. One reason why he feels lucky to be an illustrator is because he can listen to books on tape while he works. Mike is available to provide custom illustrations for all manner of publications at reasonable prices. Mike can be reached at www.mikereedillustration.com.

Free!
Oracle 10g Senior DBA Reference Poster

This 24 x 36 inch quick reference includes the important data columns and relationships between the DBA views, allowing you to quickly write complex data dictionary queries.

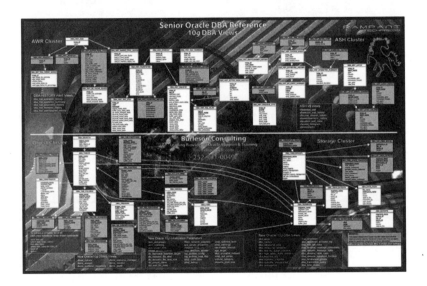

This comprehensive data dictionary reference contains the most important columns from the most important Oracle10g DBA views. Especially useful are the Automated Workload Repository (AWR) and Active Session History (ASH) DBA views.

WARNING - This poster is not suitable for beginners. It is designed for senior Oracle DBAs and requires knowledge of Oracle data dictionary internal structures. You can get your poster at this URL:

www.rampant.cc/poster.htm